By the Grace of God

The Story of Reverend Lars E. Green

*Norwegian Immigrant and Pioneering Pastor
To Southern Minnesota's
Brown & Watonwan Counties*

By Kristen S. Moore

OTTERHOUSE
BOOKS

Cover Photo of Lars E. Green, from *Norsk lutherske prester i Amerika, 1843-1913.* Augsburg Publishing House, Minneapolis, MN. 1914. Library of Congress, Public Domain.

Cover Design by Kristen S. Moore via canva.com

Edited by E. Maxwell Moore.

ISBN: 979-8-9921446-0-4 (Paperback)
Library of Congress Control Number: 2025937310
First Edition Printing, 2025.

OTTERHOUSE
BOOKS

100 North Howard Street, Suite R
Spokane, WA 99201

otterhousebooks.com

Table of Contents

For My Grandpa, Rolf Green

Rolf Green, age 90. Photo Credit: Cindy Green, 2022

*T*his book was inspired by a miraculous discovery I made in 2022 while researching my grandfather's genealogy for his ninetieth birthday celebration.

I was adopted as an infant and knew nothing of my biological roots prior to 2011. This is when I learned the original name on my birth certificate, "Baby Girl Green," and when I first met my Green family. I quickly formed a very close relationship with my maternal grandfather, and I feel so blessed to have him in my life. I adore our time together and try to absorb as much of him as I can. I cherish the stories he tells of growing up in Norway and of his many life adventures.

My grandfather, Rolf Green, was born in Norway in 1932, and immigrated to the United States as a newlywed in 1954. At only twenty-two years old, he and my grandmother, Unni, had only $100 in their pockets when they arrived in New York Harbor. My grandparents started out with nothing, but through hard work and perseverance they achieved the American Dream and created a long, prosperous and happy life for themselves in Seattle, Washington.

As I researched Grandpa Rolf's line, I uncovered a previously unknown family story. It turns out he wasn't the first Green to make the voyage across the Atlantic from Norway to America. Through my research, our family learned for the first time that my still-living grandfather had uncles, aunts, and cousins immigrate to the United States in the nineteenth century.

These original Green immigrants all settled in and around Hanska, Minnesota—a tiny prairie village with a current population of approximately 380 people. Astonishingly, Hanska is the very same town that I, on a whim, moved my family to in 2006 when we were looking for a change and a slower pace of life. My husband, our two young sons, and our family cat left our West Coast lives behind and set off cross-country toward a tiny Midwestern town we'd never heard of. Although we only lived there for one year before moving back to the Seattle area—somehow, something had pulled me to Hanska.

When people ask us how we chose Hanska, of all places, we always joke that we basically spun the globe and wherever our finger landed was where we'd go. We could never have imagined that the house we purchased, after seeing only a picture of it, was two blocks from the original homestead of Gustav Green, Rolf's great-uncle. We picked up mail every day from the post office on land that once belonged to Gustav. Rolf's other great-uncle, Reverend Lars Green, had a forty-year-long career preaching at the area's Norwegian Lutheran churches. One of the churches he preached at, Zion Lutheran, was just one street over from our home. We could regularly hear the church bells ring. Two other churches were less than three miles from our Hanska address—Lake Hanska Lutheran and Linden Lutheran. And, two more were approximately ten miles away—Trinity Lutheran in Madelia and Our Saviour's Lutheran in Butternut. We were, literally, in the center of the cluster of Lutheran churches once known as "The Green Parish."

We attended services at Nora Unitarian Universalist Church, just a mile and a half away from our house, not knowing that Green relatives were laid to rest in the church cemetery mere steps from where we sat in the pews. Our backyard faced a cornfield—within that cornfield was Zion Lutheran Cemetery, a half mile from our house. Within that cemetery, even more Green relatives were laid to rest. Houses that were built by and lived in by Green relatives stood only blocks away from our home.

There are nearly two billion acres of land in the United States. And somehow, perhaps through divine intervention, I chose a home in a tiny town that, unbeknownst to me, had been settled by my family members 125 years earlier. We were unknowingly living amongst the remnants of their American dreams and their pioneer lives. I unknowingly walked in their footsteps.

This is the story about the life of my third great uncle, Revered Lars E. Green; who, like my grandfather, left Norway as a young man to pursue his own American Dream, following the calling to leave his homeland and seek a new life overseas. He sailed to America, became an ordained Lutheran pastor, and suffered many hardships as a pioneer. But he persisted in his calling, and helped establish several churches in southern Minnesota's Brown, Blue Earth, and Watonwan Counties. It has been my honor to share his story with you.

Norge

*T*he land of Norway was geographically formed around twelve thousand years ago when melting ice, thousands of feet thick, exposed habitable land for the first time. In the years directly following the last Ice Age, the nomadic humans of this region survived by gathering edible plants, fishing the coasts, and hunting seal, elk, and whales. The oldest skeletal remains in Norway, "Brunstad Man," is estimated to be approximately eight thousand years old. He died during the Stone Age and was discovered during a 2014 excavation in Stokke, Norway, seventy miles south of Oslo. From ancient times until today, the highest concentration of people in Norway has been centered around the Oslofjord area in the southern part of the country.

Agriculture developed approximately six thousand years ago, when inhabitants began farming barley, oats, and livestock throughout the land. This increase in food stability furthered prosperity and enabled the population to grow significantly. During this time of growth, arable land became a valuable resource. People began to form settlements and boundaries to protect their assets, especially along the warmer southern coastland and fjords.

The origins of Norse paganism can be traced back to the Iron Age, around 550 BC. It was the principal religion of the Nordic people for nearly a thousand years. In Old Norse religion, the gods and goddesses lived in Asgard, and often traveled to Earth to engage in wars with giants. Ragnarök is the name of the cataclysmic final battle between the gods and giants foretold to occur in the distant future. In this belief, the forthcoming epic battle will leave the Earth scorched and in ruins, but in time it shall renew itself once more into the beautiful planet we have today.

The Viking Era lasted from approximately 800 to 1050 AD. The Vikings followed the Old Norse pagan religion, which eventually came to an end as monks, merchants, and raiding Vikings traveled throughout Europe and learned of Christianity. Catholicism slowly began to spread throughout Scandinavia. King Olaf II, the patron saint of Norway, is credited as being the converted king who first brought the Catholic faith to Norway around 1026 AD.

In 1349, the Black Plague reached Norwegian shores on an infected trade ship that arrived in Bergen. The population was decimated. Only one third of the people survived. Twenty years later, the Bishop of Trondheim wrote to Pope Gregory IX about the horrific pandemic. He recounted that out of three hundred priests only forty survived. Norway's entire population following the Plague was approximately 200,000. It would take centuries to return to the number it had prior to the outbreak.

The Protestant Reformation of the sixteenth century swept throughout all of Europe, Norway included. Many protestant religions were formed as more people broke away from the Catholic Church. In 1537, King Christian III converted from Catholicism and made Lutheranism the official religion of both Norway and Denmark.

The people of Norway lived their lives in much the same manner as their ancestors had for several centuries. Where they made their home, what they did for a profession, and their social standing within the community were all predestined at birth. A major disruption to this social system occurred during the nineteenth century, with a mass migration from Norway to America.

This is the biography of one of those emigrants. Reverend Lars Engebretsen Green was the first of his family to leave his ancestral home for a new life in the United States. He became a pioneering pastor to many churches in southern Minnesota's Brown, Watonwan, and Blue Earth counties when he decided to devote his life to the church and to his community. His long life of selfless service left behind a legacy that impacted hundreds of Norwegian immigrant families and their thousands of descendants.

Drammen, Norway, 1930. Photo Credit: Wikimedia Commons, Public Domain.

Lofoten, Norway.
Photo Credit: www.renopenose.getarchive.net. Public Domain.

Nes Parish

Nes Church Ruins. Photo Credit: Dani Rosenblad James

*F*or hundreds of years, the Church of Norway was the only legally recognized religious body in the country. It was one of the most important instruments of power and legal authority, especially at the regional and local levels. Prior to 1845, it was impossible to leave the church. Today, children born to Norwegian citizens are automatically entered into membership, but unlike previous generations, parents and adults are now able to discontinue their membership with a signature.

Church attendance has been rapidly declining in Norway for decades. Despite record-low attendance, it wasn't until the 2017 passing of the Church Act when the separation of church and state became law. For centuries, the King of Norway was head of the church, but a 2012 constitutional amendment put an end to that tradition.

In his doctoral thesis, Sivert Skålvoll Urstad described Norway as the world's most secular country, and despite only two percent of the population regularly attending church, seventy percent still maintain membership in the Church of Norway. "The church is important as a bearer of traditions, even for the non-religious people. However, their interpretation of the tradition is different. They view the church as a secular arena for confirmation and other rites of passage such as baptisms, weddings, and funerals. To them it is not about religion, but tradition." Urstad said.

Today, church is sewn deeply into the lives of Norwegians, even though the relationship has shifted to a more cultural than spiritual connection. This was not the case when Lars Green was born in 1841. At the time of his birth, the Church of Norway had absolute authority. All baptisms, marriages, and funerals were recorded through the local church parishes and were the official legal records. These records remain an invaluable resource for today's historians and family researchers.

Of Norway's seventeen counties, Lars Green's forefathers are from Akershus County within the Romerike district east of Oslo, along the southeast coast of the North Sea. The county's most iconic structure, Akershus Fortress, was built in the 1290s to act as defense against invading Swedes, as well as a royal residence. It protected Oslo Harbor, which in turn protected all of Norway. The fortress sustained heavy damage when struck by lightning in 1527, but continued to survive every siege attempt it ever encountered.

A great fire devastated Oslo in 1624—during the rebuilding, King Christian IV ordered the new city to be built closer to Akershus Fortress, and to be renamed Christiana in honor of the king. The capital city held this new name until 1925, when it was changed back to the original name of Oslo. Akershus Fortress would go on to become the inspiration and model for Arendelle Castle in the Disney animated film *Frozen*.

Akershus County was divided into fifty parishes. Of these, Nes Parish was the home church of Reverend Green's family for centuries. The first Nes Church (pronounced "Næs Kyrkje" in Old Norse) was built out of stone in the twelfth century. As Christianity spread throughout the land, churches were often built upon pagan sites of worship, and Nes Church was no exception. It was constructed upon land previously used for ritual sacrifice by the followers of the Old-Norse religion. Næs, meaning "headland," and the broader Nes area is one of the largest producers of wheat in the country. The church was named after the old Næs farm, and the sacred site was chosen because it overlooked the joining of two rivers: the Glomma River, Norway's largest, and the Vorma River. In 1697, the church was transformed into the shape of a cross by building additions onto each side of the long, rectangular stone building.

Nes Parish was established as its own municipality in 1838. Three years later, six-week-old Lars was baptized within the thick, ancient walls of the magnificent stone dwelling just as every generation before him had been. After standing boldly on the hillsides overlooking the two rivers below for seven hundred years, Nes Church was struck by lightning in 1854. The wooden roof was burned to the ground, just as Akershus Fortress had burned three centuries prior.

Young Lars was thirteen years old at the time, and it was likely devastating to his small community. His was the last generation to have worshipped in the primitive stone church, and among the first to worship in the new one. It took six years for the community to rebuild their parish. The new Nes Church, that is still standing today, was completed in 1860. Built out of brick, the new church was located two kilometers from the original structure. It was not rebuilt on the old site due to fear of mudslides, but the original stone walls that remain at Old Nes are a national landmark. They are among the best-preserved stone church ruins in the country. The site is open for visitors year-round, and is a popular spot for picnics and weddings in the Nes region today. Of historical note is the relationship between Nes Parish and Norway's most famous painter, Edvard Munch. The uncle of the world-famous artist was Edvard Storm Munch, and he was the Nes Parish priest from 1875 to 1894.

Many religious artifacts from the ancient church were salvaged and brought to the new one where they are currently displayed. Today, it takes twelve minutes to drive from Reverend Lars' ancestral family home to where Nes Parish stands. In his day it would have been an hour-and-a-half ride by horse and carriage to attend church. When he was a young man in his twenties, and a member of the new brick church, Lars received the call to become a pastor.

Nes Kirke, Akershus County, Norway. Built in 1860.
Photo Credit: Mahlum. Wikimedia Commons Public Domain.

Grinkelsrud

*T*here is very little arable land in Norway. Today, only three percent is suitable for raising crops, and the same was true during Lars Green's time as well. The men who owned farmland belonged to an agricultural social class known as the Bønder. These upper-class farmers were amongst the most powerful and influential population of the eighteenth and nineteenth centuries. Estates (gårds) were passed from father to eldest son, and it wasn't uncommon for ownership to remain in a single-family dating back to ancient times. The Bønder class, together with the nobility and clergy, were influential in government and policymaking. During the four hundred years that Norway was ruled by Denmark, the Bønder remained free men. Familial lines that include many generations of Bønder are much easier to trace due to the paper trails. Landowners paid their taxes to the Crown, which therefore, kept accurate records of the landowners, their family, their debts and their property.

Lars Green's father belonged to the Bønder class. Each gård had a name, and his family home was a very large farm called "Grinkelsrud." Wheat was likely the farm's main crop since the southeast region of Norway, including the Nes area, was (and still is) ideal for wheat farming due to its warmer growing conditions. Many men of the Green lineage, including Lars' brothers Gustav and Bernt, became master bakers, which lends credence to Grinkelsrud having been a wheat farm.

Grinkelsrud Farm circa 1961, Norway. Photo Source: Unknown

There is an aerial photograph of Grinkelsrud, taken in 1961, that shows a bucolic scene of country life. Looking at the photo one can see the property where Lars was born and had lived until his emigration to the United States.

The photo shows two barns. The one in the forefront is made of wood and very old, built at least a hundred years from when the photo was taken, so it's possibly the barn Lars knew well. It is weathered and grayish brown, but still stands strong and proud. It has numerous open bays on the bottom for livestock or equipment storage, and there's a large hayloft on top with a long ramp connecting the loft to the ground below. A row of tall trees, planted to create a wind barrier, separates the two barns.

The second barn was built in 1947 and is enormous at nearly five thousand square feet. It's much larger than the old barn and has a high, cement foundational wall that is painted white. The top two thirds of the barn are painted red and made of wood. One section of the barn is designated as a grain-drying facility with hot-air fans and storage silos, in addition to an area for cold-air drying and a grain elevator—further evidence of Grinkelsrud having been a wheat farm for many generations.

The photo also shows an old stabbur that was used for storage next to the century-old weathered barn. A "stabbur" is a traditional building every farm in Norway had prior to the twentieth century. It's becoming rarer to find original stabburs still standing. Stabburs were two-story structures built on stilts, much smaller than barns. The top story is larger than the bottom. This particular building style acted as two levels of protection: from rodents and from the elements. Along with grain and other food stores, traditional clothing and special heirlooms were stored in the stabbur as well. The lady of the house was traditionally the keeper of the keys to the family stabbur. Because of the wealth held inside this single outbuilding, it was perfectly legal to kill, on site, any person trying to break into one.

According to Norwegian folklore, each farmstead has a Christmas gnome living in their stabbur. The Christmas gnome brings gifts for well-behaved children, but if the gnomes are not carefully looked after, they can play tricks on people. On Christmas Eve, children put out a bowl of rice porridge sprinkled with sugar and cinnamon to keep their stabbur gnome happy.

Atop the stabbur was the bell tower that kept the farm on schedule. The bell was typically only used during spring, summer, and autumn. For many, the first sound of the bell at the start of the season was a cherished sign of spring.

TalkNorway is an online resource targeted to the descendants of Norwegian emigrants. It teaches many aspects of Norwegian culture and history. The site gives an example of daily farm life and the role the bell tower played in keeping the farm's daily schedule. The following comes from the Holstad farm in Ås, Akershus, Norway, which is about an hour's drive from Grinkelsrud.

The working day began at 06:00, when the farm people tended to the domesticated animals, and milked the cows. The first bell of the day was at 08:00, when the workers were called back in for breakfast. It also tolled at 11:30 for dinner — and then again between 13:00 to 13:30 to rouse the workers from their midday rest. Later it called them home for some food at 16:00, and then lastly to mark the end of the working day at 19:00.

Prominent in the 1961 photo of Grinkelsrud is a large, white farmhouse that, based on the style, was possibly the childhood home of Lars Green. Speckled throughout the farm are smaller homes, for extended family and hired hands. The photo was taken during the autumn harvest season, as there are visible tractor wheel marks in the freshly mown fields. Other fields have golden wheat still standing, ready to be reaped. There's a pond a short distance from the front of the old gray barn that was used for watering livestock. There are three cows gently grazing in the furthest pasture, and in the far background are vast forested hills covered in evergreen trees. The photo is a timeless depiction of what life looked like not only sixty years ago, but a hundred and sixty years ago as well.

The earliest Norwegian church records date from 1624. Most christening records began in the late 1600s after King Christian's law of 1686, which made the registration of christenings mandatory for all of Norway. Because of this, it's very difficult to follow Norwegian ancestral lines prior to the late 1600s. The Green family is fortunate in that there are records showing Reverend Lars' lineage back to a grandfather born in 1560 in Akershus County. Grinkelsrud ownership within the same family can be traced back to the year 1580, but it's likely that family ownership extends even further.

Record keeping prior to this date is rare and difficult to find. For centuries Norway used a patronymic pattern of naming their children. For example, a son named "Hans" whose father was "Anders" became "Hans Andersen." Further, a daughter of "Anders" named "Mari" became "Mari Andersdatter." If the name of the family gård was "Rustad" then "Hans Andersen Rustad" would also be used. Hans' children and grandchildren would have completely different surnames, but by using the name of their gård, families remained more unified. Norwegians were inconsistent with their use of surnames as well as name spellings, and this practice followed the emigrants to the New World as well. While not an exclusive rule, the spelling of a Scandinavian surname will typically differentiate between the countries of origin—"son" for Swedish surnames and "sen" for Norwegian and Danish surnames.

Reverend Green's great-great grandfather Ole Alfsen Kommesrud was baptized at Nes Parish in 1693. Because Ole had no sons, the husband of his eldest daughter Kari was destined to inherit Ole's farm. Kari Olesdatter married Svend Svendsen of Skøyen on November 24, 1754.

Svend was born in 1735 and lived his entire life in the area surrounding Nes Parish in Akershus County, Norway. Kari and Svend had seven children together. Their eldest son Ole, named after his grandfather, was born in 1765 and baptized at Nes Parish.

In 1797, Lars' great-grandfather Svend officially handed Grinkelsrud over to his thirty-three-year-old son, Ole Svendsen. Ole married Birthe Embretsdatter, and together they had four children:

Inger, Lars, Embret, and Mathea. Their second son, Embret Olsen, was born at Grinkelsrud in 1802 and baptized at Nes Parish. He would become the father of Lars Green. In 1809, when he was seven years old, his mother passed away leaving four small children. Embret's father continued to manage the farm until 1831. In defiance of tradition, Ole divided his estate equally between his two sons, Lars and Embret.

Lars' farm became Sørgarn, which meant the southern portion of the estate, while Embret's farm was named Nordgarn, for the northern portion. As is common in Norwegian records, the recorded spellings of Embret's name are inconsistent. Some of the different spellings of his first name include: Embret, Ingebret, and Engebret. He used the surnames Olsen, Nordgarn, and Grinkelsrud, and he used them in different combinations as well.

A year after inheriting his gård, Embret married Barbro Nilsdatter at Nes Parish. Barbro was born in Eidsvoll in 1812, and was two years old when the historic signing of the Norwegian Constitution occurred at Eidsvoll Manor on May 17, 1814—the day Norway declared its independence, and is celebrated today as a commemorated national holiday. Soon after their wedding, Embret and Barbro started their own family at Grinkelsrud.

Their first child was born in 1833; a son they named Ole Nikolai in honor of his grandfather. A second son followed in 1834, who they named Bernt, followed by a daughter, Bertha, in 1837. Their fourth child was born on April 20, 1841. Embret named the child Lars, in honor of his brother.

Lars Engebretsen Green was born during the height of planting season, when the farm was coming alive in the spring after a long, cold winter. A few months before he turned three years old, the family was greeted by the birth of twin girls; Karen and Etta Birgitta in January of 1844. When Lars was five years old, Embret and Barbro's fourth and final son was born to the family in July 1846: a boy they named Gustav. Daughters Maren Olava (born 1849), Ida Aletta (born 1851) and Berte Christina (born 1854) completed the family unit.

Being of the Bønder class, the lives of the ten Grinkelsrud siblings were shielded from the ravages of poverty most children in Norway endured during that time. Life for young Lars was made easier by his family's employment of household servants and farm workers, but he and his siblings were still taught the values of hard work, fortitude, and independence.

Of the four brothers, the two oldest, Ole and Bernt, lived their entire lives at Grinkelsrud in Norway while the younger two, Lars and Gustav, both immigrated to the United States. Being the two youngest of four brothers, they knew they would never inherit the farm, and therefore decided to forge different paths for themselves. Lars was the first to make the journey.

He boarded the *Eucharis* as Lars Embretsen Grinkelsrud, but he left the entirety of his past behind him on the shores of Norway. He never again used the name of his forefathers, or the name of the family estate. Instead, he anglicized and shortened Grinkelsrud to Green, and in an act of brotherhood back home, Bernt and Gustav did the same. As did his sisters. Ole Nikolai, being the eldest Grinkelsrud heir, kept with family tradition and did not change his name. However, records show that some of his children later adopted the Green name.

After Lars departed for America, Bernt and Gustav began to officially use Green on all their documents and children's baptisms. Even Lars' father, Embret, used Green in his later years. A quick Google search shows that there are 675 people with the last name "Green" living in Norway. It is very likely that they are all the descendants of Ole and Bernt within this one family. And those with the last name "Grinkelsrud," in both Norway and the United States, are descendants of the Grinkelsrud farm.

In 2023, the 147-acre Grinkelsrud Farm of Nes, Norway sold for $794,000 USD. As this book was being written, the farm which had been in the same family for countless centuries was sold to the public for the very first time.

Grinkelsrud Farm, 2023. Photo Credit:
https://www.finn.no/realestate/businesssale/ad.html?finnkode=396162996

The Mass Migration

Arriving Immigrants to Ellis Island, New York, 1902.
Photo Credit: Library of Congress, Public Domain

*T*he huge population growth in Norway between 1800 and 1900 led to overcrowding within the social structure of the day, and was a contributing factor to the wave of emigrants leaving Norway for North America. According to the Library of Congress, no other country had more of its population immigrate during the nineteenth century than Norway. In the century between 1825 and 1925, approximately nine hundred thousand Norwegians journeyed across the Atlantic in mass migration to the United States, the largest surge occurring directly after the American Civil War. By the late 1860s, forty thousand Norwegians had made America their new home. During the 1880s alone, one ninth of the entire population of Norway immigrated to the United States.

This large exodus during the 1880s was mainly due to the economic depression within Europe at the time. Advancements in steamship technology had almost entirely replaced sailing vessels during this decade as well. This transition from sail to steam made the journey more affordable to passengers of lower socio-economic status. The majority of the ships arrived in New York Harbor, and from there most Norwegian immigrants headed to the plains of Minnesota and Wisconsin. They were lured by the Homestead Act of 1862 and its promise of free farmland—a scarcity in Norway. A smaller percentage headed even further west to the Pacific Northwest. Outside of the state of Minnesota, the Seattle area holds the next highest Norwegian cultural presence.

The immigrants to the new world settled in recently developed towns and communities that had clusters of other Norwegians who had arrived before them—often friends and family from their former communities back home. The settlers encountered many hardships on the unforgiving plains, including difficulty assimilating, continued poverty, crop failure, and sickness. It is estimated that thirty percent of the Norwegians who emigrated made the decision to leave their new lives and voyage back home to Norway.

A study from UC Davis in 2016 found that the Norwegians who returned to Norway during the late nineteenth century became more prosperous after returning home than they would have been had they never left. In part, they were able to use the savings they made in the U.S. to buy cheap land or to increase their social status in poverty-stricken Norway.

The U.S. Immigration Act of 1924 nearly put a stop the Age of Mass Migration from Europe. The law put a quota on the number of immigrants allowed to enter. It figured into account each nationality listed in the 1890 census and began limiting the number of annual visas to only two percent of what was recorded in the census. For example, if there were 100,000 German-born individuals listed in the 1890 U.S. Census then only 2,000 visas for German nationals would be approved per year after the act was passed.

The number of Norwegian immigrants trickled to only a few thousand per year following the act. However, it picked up again after World War II, with approximately 22,000 immigrants arriving during the 1950s, and 17,000 during the 1960s. During the 1970s, Norwegian immigration to the United States nearly stopped following Norway's discovery of oil in the late sixties. The once poverty-stricken small nation was now on course to becoming the wealthy and prosperous leading country that it is today.

The Journey

Three-Masted Sailing Ship. Photo Credit: Library of Congress, Public Domain

*W*hen Lars Embretsen Green was born at Grinkelsrud in the spring of 1841, he became the fourth child to be welcomed into the family by his parents Embret Olsen and Barbro Nilsdatter. The long winter had ended, and the days were beginning to stretch longer and become brighter. Tiny blossoms could be seen in the meadows, birds could be heard singing in the mornings, and new life was emerging all around the farm and gardens.

Lars was born on April 20, 1841, and baptized six weeks later on June 6. He was baptized under the name Lars Ingebretsen at the old Nes Church. His infant head was cleansed with holy water at the ancient alter of the 700-year-old stone-walled church, as was every generation before him dating back to the Viking era. Lars' great-grandfather who was born in 1765, Ole Svendsen Grinkelsrud, was seventy-six years old when Lars was born. Ole died shortly after Lars' baptism. Lars was the last of Ole's great-grandchildren to be held by the patriarch of Grinkelsrud.

When Lars was thirteen years old, the medieval church burned down after being struck by lightning, and the new Nes Church wouldn't be completed until six years later in 1860. During his teenage years, the family likely worshiped at Fenstad Parish a short distance away.

Nothing is known of Lars' young life at Grinkelsrud except that he was the fourth of what would become ten children total and that he was the third of four sons. All ten children survived to adulthood. While poverty ravaged Norway during the mid-1800s, Lars' family was blessed with land ownership, and his childhood was comfortable compared to most. Family and farm life were made easier by the employment of household servants and laborers. Even though the family had help, Lars was no stranger to hard work or independence, as evidenced by his fortitude and character throughout his life. He knew farming well, and was educated in both Norwegian and English. Being the third son of the family, he knew from a young age that his older brother Ole was to be the next owner and heir of Grinkelsrud. Lars understood he would have to find other prospects.

When Lars was twenty years old, he received the calling to become a pastor. He described in a letter how God told him to "awake," and that Christ would show him the way. He began to read the Bible and pray daily. With his newfound zeal for life and the Word, he longed for everyone to experience this same grace. He spoke with whoever he could about turning from sin and to instead turn to God. He separated himself from his former friends who he referred to as "servants of sin." Lars attended local prayer groups in the area, and decided to apply to seminary in America. He wanted his life to have a higher purpose, and to be of service to others, and the best way he could think of to do so was to become a minister.

In the Norway of the nineteenth century, only those born to the higher class had the opportunity to become ministers due to the many years of academic studies in theology, reading, and writing required. In contrast, working-class men were needed for farm labor and trade work and were not able to devote themselves to years of schooling, nor had they the ability to afford it financially. Men such as Reverend Green and the many others who joined the cloth left the comforts of a privileged home to dedicate their lives to service in a poverty-stricken, desolate new land. This selfless act was a true sacrifice on their part.

A year before his intended voyage, Lars was listed in the 1865 Norwegian Census as working at Grinkelsrud. His occupation was listed as a "snedker" which translates to "carpenter." Two weeks after his twenty-fifth birthday in the spring of 1866, Lars set sail for America.

The trip from his home at Grinkelsrud to the ship's harbor in Oslo would have been a three-hour ride by horse and buggy for young Lars. He likely arrived at least one day prior and made lodging arrangements so there was no chance of him missing the departure—a departure that had been planned for years. One can imagine his emotions: excitement, hope, trepidation, and even sadness at leaving the only home and family he'd ever known, not knowing when or if he'd ever return.

The ship that brought Lars from Oslo to America was named *Eucharis*. The passenger L. E. Grinkelsrud is the fifty-second person listed on the ship manifest, and his future wife, Jensine Jensen, is the fifty-fifth passenger. Two men, on lines 53 and 54, are listed between Lars and Jensine. Both men are from Eidsvold, which is twelve miles from Grinkelsrud. It is not known if there was a connection between Lars and the two men. Having their home towns so close together could show a relationship, or just be mere coincidence.

Directly under Jensine's name on the passenger list is the Svenskerud family of nine: two parents and their seven children. Perhaps young Jensine traveled as their nanny, and she and Lars met on the journey for the first time by happenstance. Perhaps she was sailing as a single young woman and braving the voyage to the New World on her own—with her dreams of the future held tight. Or, perhaps Jensine and Lars were sweethearts who, due to class restrictions, could not marry in Norway and so decided to travel to

America together. If this were the scenario, the pair needed the two additional friends as chaperones in order to make the travel appropriate and respectable.

While the particulars will remain forever unknown, it seems likely that the two knew each other, even though Lars was of the Bønder class and Jensine was working-class poor, as shown in the 1865 census a year prior to their departure. The two were born exactly one week apart, and both of them were baptized at Nes Parish. This detail is likely not a coincidence.

Not much is known about Jensine Marie Jensen's life prior to her leaving Norway. She was born on April 28, 1841. In the 1865 Norwegian Census, she was listed as twenty-four years old. She, along with her widowed mother and three younger siblings, were living in a workhouse in Oslo, then known as Christiana. Both Jensine and her mother, Matea Jensen, list Nes Parish as the location of their baptisms. Along with the two women, the family unit consisted of Jensine's sixteen-year-old brother, Anton Sevrin, and her two younger sisters: Nekolina Gustave, age thirteen, and Ingeborg Mathea, age nine. The three younger siblings were all baptized in Christiana.

Twenty-eight tenants are listed as living at the same residence: Five families with children, and a single male gardener. Jensine's mother Matea is listed as a widow, and her occupation is "Madhandlerske Pølsekoger," which translates to "Grocer, Sausage Cooker." Jensine's occupation shows her working as a seamstress.

The struggling family lived in the district of Fjerdingens Gade, a part of Oslo known for its poorhouses. The settlement no longer remains. In 1896, Fjerdingens Gade was renamed Christian Krohg's Street. Most poorhouses of the time were on farms, and the one Jensine's family lived at was numbered "Farm 24." The head, or host, of the house is Hans Mathiesen, age sixty-nine, and his wife Karine Larsdatter, age seventy-five. Like Jensine and her mother, Karine was also baptized at Nes Parish.

Jensine's mother Matea's 1819 baptism record at Nes Parish shows her parents were Andreas Jensen and Kari Mathiesdatter.

"Mathies" was the first name of not only Matea's grandfather, but of the farm host's father as well. From this information it's likely that Matea is the niece of farm host Hans Mathiesen.

Interestingly, Matea is using her father's surname, Jensen, as are all her children. This was unusual for the time as most women and girls used the patronymic pattern of "datter" after their father's name for their surname. Using this custom, Matea and her daughters would have had different last names that ended in "datter" rather than "sen."

No record of marriage for Matea Jensen could be found, but that's not to say it doesn't exist. Records for working-class people are often difficult to obtain, especially since the only census taken prior to the 1865 one was in 1801, sixty-four years earlier. Jensen is one of the most common names in Norway, so Matea could have also married a man with the same last name as her father. Considering all the Nes connections though, it's highly feasible that Lars and Jensine knew each other prior to embarking on their journey.

The 1865 Census is the only record of Jensine in Norway. Considering she sailed for America the following year in 1866, it would have been the final record as well. The 1870 Norwegian Census shows Jensine's mother, Matea, and seventeen-year-old sister, Nekolina Gustava, living in a large house, probably a workhouse, with eighty-seven tenants. Jensine's youngest sister Ingeborg, who would have been thirteen at this time, is not with them, but no death records can be found for any of Jensine's family in Norway.

Because there's a large age difference between Jensine and her younger siblings, it's highly possibly that their mother Matea's first husband passed away, and Jensine's siblings are from a different father. Genealogy research often leaves many questions unanswered, much to the frustration of historians.

The *Eucharis*, the ship that took Lars and Jensine to America, was a three-masted sailing ship. Most immigrants at this time still arrived via sailing vessels, as steamships weren't commonplace until the 1880s. The *Eucharis*—named after the South American white lily flower—was built in 1837 at Wiffsta Warf in Sweden. It was owned by J. Risting. Her home port was Christiana (now Oslo), Norway. The ship typically carried emigrants from Norway to America only once each spring when the Atlantic Ocean conditions were safest. The rest of the year she transported lumber from Sweden to London.

A week after Jensine's twenty-fifth birthday, she and Lars began their long journey to America. As they watched the shoreline of Norway slowly disappear, they wondered if they would ever see her again. The *Eucharis* departed from Christiana on May 6, 1866, and arrived in Quebec, Canada on June 13, 1866. She was sailing in ballast, and was carrying three hundred and sixty-three Norwegian steerage passengers. She was mastered by Captain Andersen, and the passenger list was signed by Captain Nannestad. She had a crew of sixteen men. The passenger list is archived by the National Archives of Canada (NAC).

During Lars and Jensine's crossing one man died of acute rheumatism, and when the ship arrived to the quarantine station four children were sick with diarrhea. The ship was filthy and had to be detained until it could be fully cleaned and disinfected. Without a doubt there were several prayers made by everyone on board throughout the long, cramped journey. Lars, with his deep faith and on his way to seminary, likely encouraged the other passengers to keep hope as he led them in prayer. The long weeks at sea bonded the young couple and the memories of their shared, harrowing experience lasted their lifetime.

In August of 1866, the *Eucharis* set sail back to Europe after that year's immigrants disembarked, young Lars and Jensine among them. But a few weeks later, she turned around and headed back towards Plymouth, Massachusetts. The ship was leaking. After a few days of being docked in Plymouth the leak was fixed, and she resumed her voyage homeward across the ocean once again.

On December 14, 1866, an advertisement for the next transatlantic passenger crossing was posted in the Norwegian daily newspaper *Hamar Stiftstidende*. This ad was for the crossing directly after Lars and Jensine's voyage, but it's likely identical to the announcement Lars read when he was planning his own voyage. It announced the 1867 spring sailings aboard the *Eucharis* and her sister ship the *Dagmar.* Accompanying the ad was a drawing of the three-masted ship with its billowing, full sails. It stated that the *Eucharis* crossed in thirty-four days the year prior, and it showed that the fees per passenger were to be paid in silver coins.

These coins, Speciedaler, were replaced in 1874 by the monetary system currently used today in Norway, the Kroner. The fee for an adult passenger was listed at 15 Speciedaler. 8 Speciedaler was the price for children ages eight to fourteen, and 5 Speciedaler was the price for children between one and eight years old. There was an additional 1 Speciedaler added as a landing fee for each passenger. The equivalencies to today's U.S. dollar would be approximately $907 per adult, $479 for older children, and $300 for small children. The ad further stated that private cabins were available, and that an interpreter would follow the passengers all the way to Chicago. During the prior year's journey in 1866, several of the passengers departed in Quebec, but Lars and Jensine traveled the entirety of the voyage to Chicago, Illinois—where Lars then enrolled in the Swedish Lutheran Seminary in Paxton.

In May of 1866, Lars first stepped onto the wooden planks of the *Eucharis* when he boarded the ship as Lars E. Grinkelsrud. When he took his first step onto American soil, he was a changed man—his own man. He had left not only his family and ancestral home behind him, perhaps never to return, but he also left his name. It was carried away in the winds as he stood on the deck of the *Eucharis*, the same winds that propelled him forward towards his new life. He would never again use the name Grinkelsrud. From that day on, he chose to forever be known as Lars E. Green.

Unknown preacher giving a sermon onboard. *S.S. Hellig Olav*, 1905.
Photo Credit: Wikimedia Commons, Public Domain

Seminary

Augustana Seminary, Paxton, Illinois. Date unknown.
Photo Credit: https://www.augie.edu/about/history-augustana

*W*hen the Swedish Lutheran Seminary first opened its door to students on September 1, 1860, that door was attached to a single two-story, wood-framed school-house. The building sat behind the Immanuel Swedish Lutheran Church in Chicago at the intersection of Wells and Superior streets. Classes were taken in the schoolhouse as well as in the basement of the Immanuel Lutheran Church. Twenty-one students enrolled that first year in 1860: ten Swedish, ten Norwegian, and one American. Although these numbers were small, enrollment dropped even further during the mid-1860s, but picked up again after the American Civil War ended in the spring of 1865.

In 1861, the school sought a more permanent location where it could expand and attract more students. In 1863, the board of directors purchased land near Paxton, Illinois, moved the school there, and incorporated it under the name Augustana College and Seminary.

Unlike its former campus in bustling Chicago, Paxton was a quiet and remote small town, with a very large Swedish population, the majority of whom were employed in trades and services. Most of the students at Augustana were poor. The Swedish citizens of Paxton often helped the students with money and food when they could. When Lars Green attended, over half of the students received free room and board. Tuition was $10 for those who could afford it. Students who were members of the local church congregation were charged half price and students such as Lars, who were studying for the Lutheran ministry, were not charged at all.

Lars was one of the foreign students who had waited until the end of the Civil War that ravaged the United States before making his departure to seminary. His freshman year, during the fall of 1866, included fourteen other young men for a total of fifteen students. Approximately eighty men, all of whom dreamed of becoming pastors, made up the entirety of the seminary student body. It took between three and four years for each student to complete his training. The men were a close-knit group of varying ages and stages in life who all knew each other, looked out for each other, and lived and learned as brothers.

A few months before Lars' freshmen class arrived, Augustana's first library was established in the spring of 1866. Its creation was only made possible when King Charles XV of Sweden gifted 5,000 books to the school. The books had a wide range of topics including history, religion, Scandinavian culture, and French studies. Lars was among the first students who benefited from the King's generous gift.

Daily life at Augustana began at 5am. Students were expected to help with chores prior to beginning lessons. Courses, church services, and prayer meetings were all presented in Swedish, but the Norwegian students had little trouble understanding the language that was very similar to their own.

The campus eventually consisted of six wood-framed buildings, all serving double duty as both classroom space and living quarters for students and faculty. Each building was given a nickname by the students. Pastor T. N. Hasselquist, the school's president, was an admirable man who was respected by all the students. He was referred to as "The Doctor." His residence was called "Asgard"—the home of Odin, the chief god of Old Norse mythology. The dining hall where the students had their meals was "Valhalla," and the smokehouse was "Ragnarök." The building where the men took their final exams was dubbed "Purgatory."

All of the buildings were sparsely and plainly furnished. Classrooms were small and cramped. The teachers sat at simple, unadorned tables, and students sat on hewn board benches. Graduating students warned incomers about the quality of food. Bread, butter, molasses, coffee, and water were served for both breakfast and dinner. Lunch was the largest meal of the day. In addition to bread, butter, and molasses, the students were given small servings of meat, eggs, peas, and beans. A cow was eventually purchased, following repeated requests from the students who longed for milk.

Swedish church members often invited students into their homes for homemade meals and company. In addition to their studies, many students took on small jobs for extra money. President Hasselquist invited students who didn't go home over the Christmas break to his house to enjoy the holiday together. The students played sports and practiced fencing with wooden swords, and some formed a band. Debate and long conversations were held in "Ragnarök," often long into the night. A literary society, formed in 1860 in Chicago, provided the Friday night entertainment, with debate, oratory, and music on the agenda.

Even though the young men worked long hours on their studies, which took up most of their time, Lars and Jensine somehow found time to see each other. Students were not allowed to be seen holding hands with a lady as they walked about town, as this was considered sinful. It's unknown where Jensine lived during Lars' three years in seminary. She had undoubtedly gone to work as a young single woman, and found lodgings either on her own or with a family as a maid or nanny. The Svenskerud family, whose names were directly under hers in the ship manifest, had settled in Wisconsin.

After three years of dedicated study, Lars E. Green officially became a pastor of the Lutheran faith when he was ordained on November 8, 1869. The date marked another, perhaps even more special occasion. Later that same day, after Lars took his vows to become a minister, he and Jensine made their wedding vows to each other as well. It had been three and a half years since the couple voyaged to America together—three and a half years of courtship in between studies and very hard work.

At last Lars and Jensine were officially declared husband and wife, and would never need to be separated again. The combination of Lars' graduation day with his marriage day was practical as well. All of Lars' classmates, professors, and friends were already present. The men he'd shared dorms with, broke bread with, laughed and cried with were gathered as one. Soon they would all be scattered throughout the country with their own pastoral calls. The happy couple wanted to make certain to share the joyous day with their friends, especially since their families were so far away. The newlyweds were both twenty-eight years old when they exchanged their vows.

For reasons unknown, the marriage between Lars and Jensine is recorded in the Scandinavian Evangelical Lutheran Church of Milwaukee on November 8, 1869. The entries are all hand-written in black ink, and in chronological order. Interestingly, the location of the marriage is listed as "Milwaukee" as well, but is then crossed out with a single black line and "Chicago" is written above it. With the exception of only a few, all the other marriage locations are listed as "Milwaukee." There are a couple different possibilities.

In 1869, the Norwegian contingent of the original Augustana College and Seminary withdrew to Marshall, Wisconsin, when the Norwegians decided to separate from the Swedes and form their own synod and seminary. The Norwegians purchased a building in Marshall, Wisconsin, outside of Milwaukee, and in 1869 formed the Augsburg Seminary and Marshall Academy. A few months later, in 1870, the Norwegian Augustana Synod was founded, with Lars as one of its first members. Perhaps he was caught in the in-between times. Another theory is that the church he was a member of in Chicago,

Immanuel Lutheran, could have been the original location of their marriage, but because the entire church burned to the ground in the Chicago Fire of 1871, all of its records were destroyed and were being re-recorded into the new synod book.

In 1870, the number of campus buildings at Augustana Seminary doubled when a new library, lecture hall, and student dormitory were built. Later that same year, the Norwegians formally left the Scandinavian Evangelical Lutheran Augustana Synod and formed the Norwegian Augustana Synod. This synod continued to evolve and combine with other synods throughout the decades, before eventually becoming the Evangelical Lutheran Church in America (ELCA), as it remains today.

After less than a decade in Paxton, Illinois, it became clear that the town was failing to attract new Scandinavian Lutherans as was its goal. The wave of Swedish immigrants was moving north into Minnesota, or west into Nebraska and Kansas. In 1873, a few years after Lars graduated, the seminary in Paxton, Illinois moved once again, this time to Rock Island, Illinois, two hundred miles away, where it remains and continues to thrive today as a private Lutheran liberal-arts college.

Augustana Seminary, Marshall, Wisconsin. Date Unknown. Photo Credit:
https://www.augie.edu/sites/default/files/shared/The_Augustana_First50.pdf

One of the college buildings at Augusta College, Paxton, Illinois. Date Unknown.
Photo Credit:
https://www.augustana.net/SpecialCollections/timeline/paxton_image.html

Above: Map of Minnesota with the approximate area served by Reverend Green circled in black.

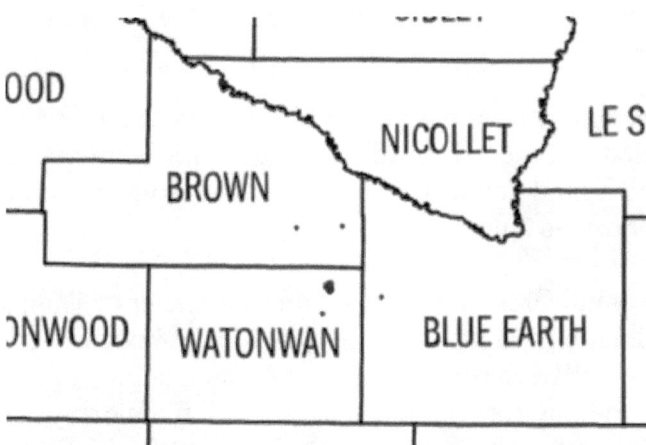

Above: The large black dot represents the location of Reverend Green's farm. The small dots represent the four churches of the Green Parish. The bordering river is the Minnesota River.

*W*anamingo, Minnesota is a small township in rural Goodhue County founded by Norwegian immigrants. The settlers of the town had been without a church since they had first arrived over a decade earlier, and they were ready to establish an official church for their community. Wanamingo Lutheran Church was first organized in July 1869, and its first officers were elected shortly after.

The primary task of the newly elected men was to select their first pastor, and Reverend Lars E. Green was their choice. He was young and still in seminary at the time, but directly after his graduation in November of 1869, he and Jensine hastened northward towards little Wanamingo. They had to race the first snowfall and arrive before the harsh Minnesota winter made travel impossible. The trip took them between ten and twelve days. During the long, cold journey the honeymooners were finally able to relax, talk at length, and enjoy the quietness and solitude of the prairie that stretched for endless miles in all directions. Once in Goodhue County, Lars stopped in the town of Red Wing, the county seat, to officially file his ordination credentials, before continuing the remaining twenty-eight-mile stretch to Wanamingo.

In December, the month following their arrival, Wanamingo Lutheran purchased two acres of land from Henry and Eliza Brown for $100. Construction began a few months later in the spring of 1870.

That summer, nine months after their marriage, Lars and Jensine welcomed their first child into the world on what was likely a very hot and humid day in Wanamingo, Minnesota. Anna Emelia Green was born on August 22, 1870.

Reverend Green only stayed on as minister of Wanamingo Lutheran Church for a little over a year. It's not known if there were irreconcilable differences between pastor and congregation, or if he was simply looking for something new and left amicably. Either way, in 1871, when little Annie was only a few months old, Reverend Green answered a new call and the young family left Wanamingo. He served briefly in Spring Valley, Minnesota before heading south to Forest City, Iowa.

The couple packed their buggy, and with baby Annie safe in Jensine's arms, the three of them set off on the hundred-mile journey. Reverend Lars was again selected to be the first pastor of a newly formed Norwegian church. This time it was Luther Lutheran Church in Forest City, Iowa. They were a new congregation, incorporated on May 10, 1870, within the Norwegian Augustana Synod. Ironically, Luther Lutheran is now Immanuel Lutheran, the same name as the church Revered Green belonged to when he was in seminary back in Paxton, Illinois.

While Reverend Green was pastor at Luther Lutheran, he and Jensine's second child was born in 1872. The couple named her Marie Josephine. The reverend stayed on as pastor of Luther Lutheran in Iowa for two years, before receiving his third call. In February of 1873, he was asked to serve the many Norwegian settlers in south-central Minnesota who were in need of a new pastor. Once the snow melted in April 1873, Lars and Jensine, with their two little girls, packed their single buggy and headed north, back to Minnesota. They did not return to Goodhue County, but instead were called to a more southern location, the tri-county area of Brown, Blue Earth, and Watonwan Counties.

Reverend Green had been called to replace Revered Thor Hattrem, who, at forty-two years old, had died of typhus during the great blizzard of January 1873 just a few months earlier. Reverend Hattrem had originally come from Lier, Buskerud County in Norway, and had immigrated in September 1869, six months after Lars Green. He brought with him his wife and two children, and the family was only in America for a few years before he tragically passed.

The journey from Iowa to Minnesota took Lars and Jensine three days. Their single buggy, carrying the entire family and all their worldly possessions, was pulled by their beloved pony named "Kab."

As the buggy traveled the desolate prairie roads of Minnesota, they were exposed to several potential hardships. Not much could be done to protect the family from the cold, wind, and rain. They were also helpless to any threats from passersby who may have had ill intent. Ten years before the Greens' arrival, the US–Dakota War of

1862 had brought terror to the area. The Battle of New Ulm, also known as the New Ulm Massacre, took place twelve miles from where Reverend Green was called to serve.

The Dakota of the area were starving due to the corruptness of the Indian agents, who refused to relinquish the agreed payments and provisions to the tribe. This was coupled with the Homestead Act of 1862, which took even more reservation land away from the Dakota people and gave it to white settlers.

In August of 1862, the Dakota turned hostile at their mistreatment. Local farmers raced to the town of New Ulm for protection. Dozens of European settlers were killed in New Ulm when the Dakota attacked, and the settlers who remained on their homesteads were helpless to any bands passing through. A few Norwegian farmers in Linden were warned by their Dakota friends and were spared from death. When it was over, over six hundred settlers, mostly unarmed, and one hundred Dakota Sioux were killed.

The New Ulm Massacre was the deadliest attack on white settlers by Native Americans in American history. The Norwegian settlements south of New Ulm were, for the most part, not attacked during the war, with one exception.

When news of the attacks spread, Ole Sorbel opened his doors to fleeing neighbors seeking refuge. One of the neighbors who gathered at Sorbel's place was Sigri Torgrimson, who was heavily pregnant. Sigri gave birth that night. The child that was born, a son she named Martin, would live to be one hundred years old. A few weeks later, Ole Sorbel gathered with neighbors to learn how to use government-issued guns for defense, when they heard a shot on the western shore of Linden Lake. When they arrived to John Armstrong's farm, they found him with an arrow in his back. His fingers, the ones that held his gun, had been chopped off. A bloody moccasin indicated that John Armstrong had been able to fight before he fell.

The following spring, the Dakota Expulsion Act of 1863 was passed. This law banished all Dakota tribal members from the state of

Minnesota, regardless of whether or not they had participated in the war. The governor of Minnesota put a bounty on the scalps of any remaining Dakota. The act has never been officially repealed, although it is no longer enforced.

Ten years after the uprising, when Reverend Green and Jensine traveled across the plains, there was no longer fear of attacks by Native Americans. There was only a slight chance of attacks by bandits, but a much more likely attack by the weather.

Like Wanamingo, the area Reverend Green was headed to serve was a cluster of townships settled by Norwegians who had first arrived in the late 1850s. These townships were approximately twelve miles south of New Ulm. New Ulm was founded by German immigrants in 1854, and when Reverend Green arrived, it had a population of approximately two thousand residents. The German language, culture, architecture, and influences of New Ulm are still heavily present and celebrated today.

Twelve miles to the south, it was the Norwegian people who populated the prairie. With them they brought their own language, culture, customs, and religious practices. Compared to the larger, neighboring town of New Ulm, the Norwegian communities were much smaller in population, and more widely spread out. Reverend Green's destination was an area on the map where three county corners met; Brown, Watonwan, and Blue Earth.

The first Norwegian settler to Brown County was Andrew Lundberg from Hurdalen, who settled in Linden in 1857. A few years later came other Norwegians who had originally settled in Wisconsin, but soon after moved east to Minnesota. Linden, named for the numerous linden trees in the area, was the center for the incoming Norwegian settlers, and was the location of the first Norwegian Lutheran Church in Brown County. The early settlers in Butternut, Madelia, Riverdale, and Lake Hanska all belonged to the Linden Congregation, which encompassed a very large area. Linden lies in the southeast corner of Brown County, in close proximity to the other two counties.

The word Hanska fittingly has both Norwegian and Native American meaning. In Norwegian, Hanska means "glove," and in the Dakota Sioux language it means "long," to represent the long, thin lake that bears its name. Furthermore, one end of Lake Hanska has been said to resemble a mitten, hence "glove" being appropriate as well.

The first Norwegian settlers to Watonwan County were Hans Johnson and John Anderson, who settled in Odin in 1856. Their only neighbors were the Dakota Sioux, and the settler's children became immersed in the Sioux language by playing with Native children. The first Norwegians to settle near Madelia consisted of approximately a dozen men who originally had settled outside of Waukesha, Wisconsin, but later moved to Minnesota, as many other southern Minnesota Norwegian settlers had done as well.

Dugouts and log cabins were their first residences. Ole Reinert, an early settler of Butterfield wrote,

As old and as forgetful as I am, I can never forget what we went through in the first years we were on these prairies. One can guess at the long trips we had with oxen — with no roads or bridges — in rain and snow storms. If there had not remained a bit of Viking blood in our veins, the hardships would have been unendurable.

The first Norwegian settlers to Blue Earth County were from the Øyer Parish area of Oppland County, Norway. In 1857, they settled in Butternut Valley, very close to Linden.

With reliable "Kab" leading the way, Reverend Green arrived in early April of 1873, just prior to Holy Week and the Easter celebration. He was greeted by Jens Torson, a fellow Norwegian and the Watonwan County Treasurer, who gave the reverend a ride to Lake Hanska. They were headed to the farm of Frantz Lee, where the Green family stayed for a few days in preparation for the reverend's first sermon in Albin.

Jens Torson was originally from Nes, Norway, just as Reverend Green was, so it's not impossible that the men knew each other back home, and had much to discuss and catch up about on the wagon ride. There was little time to rest though, as Reverend Green got straight to work with his pastoral duties. In a letter he penned during his retirement, the reverend wrote about his first days in the tri-county area:

Maundy Thursday I was to preach in Albion, a short ways from Lee's, but Lee's house was on an island surrounded by a nine-mile long lake and also a big slough, so we had to drive five extra miles to get around the slough and also back again. Well, we started out. Lee had a very good team of horses and we wanted to get over the end of the lake and there was deep water. When we got out in the middle of the lake the wagon box floated up and the water flowed over us, but the horses ran with us four men, Lee, Erick Sweine, Syver Sourgumgaard and me — Four Haugianere*— A good company. We arrived safely.

After the Easter holiday, the Green family temporarily made their home at the Nels C. Rukke farm, which later became the Henry Melzer farm. This farm was located in Brown County, Linden Township, Section 27, and the residence was located on the east side of the northwest quarter. A current plat map shows the address as 12593 State Highway 257. During his time at this residence, he was less than a two-mile ride to Linden Lutheran Church, a short commute which was likely much appreciated.

* The Haugean movement, or Haugeanism (Norwegian: haugianere), was a Pietistic-state church reform movement intended to bring new life and vitality into the Church of Norway, which had been often characterized by formalism and lethargy. The movement emphasized personal diligence, enterprise and frugality.

Reverend Green was a welcome replacement to the highly respected Reverend Hattrem, whose sudden passing left a huge void within the community. Any pastor who would have taken over the role had large shoes to fill, as well as a large area to serve, as Revered Green was the only pastor within a thirty-mile area. He performed baptisms, marriages, and funerals for not only Norwegians, but Swedes and Germans as well. Life was extremely difficult for the settlers, all of whom were poor and struggled to grow enough food to survive on their homesteads.

Before official church buildings were built on the prairie, services were conducted in the homes of the congregation members. Reverend Green's first service in Rosendale was conducted in the log cabin of a Swedish immigrant. In his letter written during retirement he recounted his first sermon at Rosendale:

On my first trip to Rosendale I fell into the cellar. I conducted services in a little log house belonging to a Swedish man. Five or six children were to be baptized, when the fathers and mothers came inside, the house was full and the rest of the people had to stand outdoors and listen as best they could. I had gotten into my ministerial garb and sung a hymn verse. "See Children are the Lord's Gift." I stood there and talked to the mothers, that they should thank God that they were well again and able to come to services with their children, to let them through baptism become members of God's Kingdom. I admonished them to pray for their children, teach them God's word, and live as a good example for them. Then the floor fell down into the cellar. The cellar was full of water so the floor floated on the water and the stove stood slanting. Men outdoors heard the crashing and came to see what was the matter. Well, we stopped a while, then continued our services with the floor floating on the water. That took two or three hours.

Soon after that event, the local schoolhouse served as both school and church. Reverend Green preached at the first official church service in a dedicated building in May of 1873. Rather than reside with area farmers as the previous pastor had, Reverend Lars was the first pastor of the parishes to have a parsonage—a private home for himself and his growing family.

Having lost their last pastor so tragically, the people of the congregation agreed that their new one needed his own lodging. A dilapidated storage house, with many rat holes and in need of much repair, was selected. Lars and Jensine were extremely grateful for this dwelling, though it was very cold. They were even more grateful when the men of the community worked together to transform it into a solid and safe home.

Many Norwegian settlements throughout the area, not just Reverend Green's main congregations, were also in need of a pastor. Once a month, he traveled many miles to preach to as many of them as he could. His week started with a trip to Albin on Monday morning, then to St. James that evening. Tuesdays he visited St. Olaf, and Wednesdays were spent at Long Prairie. He rested on Thursdays, before preaching in Rosendale on Fridays. He arrived home on Saturday in time to preach at both Linden and Madelia on Sundays.

After Reverend Hattrem's tragic passing during the blizzard of 1873, Revered Green took charge of both Our Saviour's and South Branch's congregations as well. These two later merged to become Rosendale Lutheran Church in 1877. During his first winter in the tri-county area, the reverend organized and founded the Norwegian Lutheran Church at St. James on December 28, 1873.

As the homesteaders were slowly able to build church buildings and move away from services being held in homes, Reverend Green was present for the formation and dedication of many of them. Norwegian Lutheran at St. James chose the following charter members: Henry Berntsen, Hans Olsen and Iver Olsen. The congregations of St. Olaf, Butterfield, Rosendale, Long Lake, and Albion were all combined into one, having the same pastor and same parsonage.

Two months after Reverend Green arrived to the area, Minnesota's historic grasshopper plague of 1873 began. On a warm June day, every farmer in his field heard a massive roar coming from the sky, and with it a darkened cloud advancing directly towards them. A swarm of locusts then descended into the fields and ate everything in sight. A few lucky fields were spared from the ravenous insects, but most were not. The farmers tried to beat the grasshoppers away from their fields to no avail.

The following summer, in 1874, it was even worse. The millions of eggs the grasshoppers had laid deep into the Minnesota soil the previous year had hatched and they resumed havoc upon the fields. Farmers raised birds and chickens to help control the population. They dug ditches, filled them with coal, and lit them on fire in hopes the smoke would deter them, but nothing helped. The farmers received little, if any, monetary relief from the government. This disaster would continue for four years. Just as suddenly as they had arrived, the grasshoppers abruptly ascended into the sky and left during the summer of 1877. After four years of devastation, many farmers who were already struggling to grow enough food to feed their families were now almost destitute.

From Petra Lien's writings on the history of the Lake Hanska area:

The grasshopper years of 1873–1878 is also reflected in the material progress of our church. These insects ate everything that grew in people's fields—crops, weeds and all. When people didn't get crops, they were very poor and some of the pioneers said if they had enough money to get back to Norway, they certainly would have gone. Financial help was received from the synod for poor people, the song leader, and minister's salary. However, the Reverend Green repeatedly cancelled the congregation's debt to him.

Reverend Lars and Jensine, lovingly called "Jennie" by friends and family, also had their financial struggles. The people of the community, being so poor, had very little to offer as a minister's salary. For performing baptisms, weddings, and confirmations he received $1.00, if the people could pay. Funerals were performed for free, and special collections for the pastor were taken at Easter and Christmas. Sometimes the reverend was paid in eggs or produce or with IOU checks.

It has been well-documented by different sources that Reverend Green was known to privately share his entire salary amongst struggling families within his congregations, or to refuse payment for services. Being away for long days and often overnights, he found a local boy to stay at the house to tend to the chores and animals, while Jennie was busy with the two toddlers, and expecting another little one as well.

On May 1, 1874, three days after Jensine's thirty-third birthday, she and Lars welcomed their third daughter into the world. Annie was four years old, and little Marie was two, when their baby sister Valborg Wilhelmine arrived on May Day, a day of celebrating the coming summer and beautiful warm weather. With his family continuing to grow, it was time for Reverend Green to purchase his own farm.

Sometime around 1875, the good pastor bought his own property, known as the "Green Farm," in Madelia Township in Watonwan County. The farm was located at Section 15, in the center of the township on the west side of the road. The current address is: 28557 State Highway 15. Today, the property is a private residence and no longer a working farm. The original farmhouse is gone, replaced decades ago by a large modern house that sits at the end of a long dirt driveway. The current house sits in the middle of a large lot of manicured green grass with beautifully landscaped flowers, all of which is bordered by a bright-white, split-rail fence, which marks the property line. Surrounding the property is hundreds of acres of corn fields—the same as it was during Reverend Green's time.

He couldn't have chosen a more perfect location. His home was centrally located amongst his four main congregations: four miles to Linden Lutheran and nine miles to Lake Hanska Lutheran, both in Brown County; two miles to Trinity Lutheran in Watonwan County, and ten miles to Butternut Valley's Our Saviour's Lutheran in Blue Earth County.

Soon after the Green family moved into their own house, Jennie's sister Nekolina came to live with them. Lena, as she was called, was thirteen years old the last time the two sisters saw each other in Norway. She is listed in the 1870 Norwegian Census as living with her mother in a work house in Oslo. Absent from the family are twenty-one-year-old brother Anton and fourteen-year-old sister Ingeborg. No records can be found on any of Jensine's family members in Norway after 1870. Yet we know Lena arrived to Madelia, because her gravestone lists the year of passing: 1875.

Young Lena was only twenty-two years old when she passed. She lived an impoverished childhood in Norway, and dreamed of joining her older sister in America. She traveled solo across the ocean, with her entire future ahead of her. She longed for a life of opportunity, and was filled with such promise and hope, but sadly it wasn't meant to be. She died soon after arriving, her cause of death unknown.

Jennie was pregnant when Lena died. When their fourth daughter was born on February 6, 1876, the couple named her after Jennie's dearly departed sister. Lena Eliza was baptized at Trinity Lutheran in Madelia by her father. With four little girls under the age of six to care for, Jennie was kept very busy tending to the never-ending day-to-day needs of her family.

Losing Lena so soon after she arrived to America was very difficult for Jennie and Reverend Green, but the following year would prove even more tragic. Three weeks after baby Lena was born, their daughter Marie, not yet four years old, died of scarlet fever.

The *Madelia Times* wrote the following in their March 3, 1876 edition:

At the Lutheran parsonage, in this village at 5 o'clock p.m. on Tuesday, Feb. 29, 1876, after a brief illness Marie Josefine, daughter of Rev. L. E. and Jensine Green, aged three and a half years. The Savior has thus taken another of his lambs to His arms, as He has said, "Suffer little children to come unto me and forbid them not for of such is the kingdom of Heaven." These bereaved parents have the sympathy of the community for their great loss.

Just weeks after welcoming the birth of one daughter, Lars and Jensine were forced to mourn the passing of another. Adding to the devastation, baby Lena also passed away six months later, on August

25, 1876 of "cholera infantium." Very rare nowadays, cholera infantium was a sudden sickness that affected infants and toddlers. The disease was non-contagious, but it caused severe diarrhea, vomiting, and wasting. It was common in the summer months within congested areas of high humidity and high temperatures.

Within one year's time, Lars and Jensine lost a sister and two of their four daughters. The departed little girls and their aunt were originally buried at Linden Lutheran Cemetery, but several decades later extended family moved them to Trinity Lutheran Cemetery in Madelia so they could rest eternally alongside their parents.

Perhaps one of the most historically significant experiences of Reverend Green's time happened a month after baby Lena Eliza was laid to rest. On September 21, 1876, members of the Jesse James and Younger Brothers gang were apprehended outside of Hanska in what is known at the Battle of Hanska Slough. Jennie was pregnant again, four months along. Little Annie had just turned six, and baby Valborg was two. They had no idea that one of America's most famous outlaws would travel directly past their farm one morning while being pursued by the law.

On September 7, 1874, eighty miles outside of Madelia, Jesse James, his brother Frank, along with the Younger Brothers—Cole, Jim, and Bob—Charlie Pitts, Clell Miller, and Bill Stiles attempted to rob the First National Bank of Northfield, Minnesota, but their efforts were quickly thwarted. Miller and Stiles were killed in the bank robbery, and the remaining gang members were wounded as they fled in desperation to escape the law. For weeks they were able to stay one step ahead of their pursuers as they stole horses and supplies along the way.

They traveled west towards Mankato in Blue Earth County. Near Lake Crystal, between Mankato and Madelia, the gang was recognized one night as they traveled along the back roads. They were fired upon, but managed to escape yet again. A chase immediately ensued, but law enforcement didn't realize that the gang had split in two. Only Jesse and Frank James were followed by the posse as the other outlaws fled towards South Dakota. The three Younger Brothers and Charlie Pitts continued in the opposite direction towards Hanska, Minnesota.

Weeks before the robbery, the gang had come through the Madelia–Hanska area when they were scoping out locations. They stayed at the Flanders House and asked many questions about the area, raising suspicions of the landlord, Colonel Thomas Vought. Weeks later, when news of the robbery reached Madelia, Vought immediately realized that his prior guests were the culprits. He speculated that they might return to the area, specifically to a certain bridge they had previously inquired about. Colonel Vought, along with two other men, laid in wait at the bridge for two nights.

As they waited, the men were often visited by a teenage boy who lived nearby, Asle Sorbel, known as "Oscar." The boy had been a toddler during the Battle of New Ulm, and it was his father Ole's house that the neighbors had gathered together at for safety during the height of the battles. The Sorbel Family were Norwegian immigrants who attended Linden Lutheran Church, and Reverend Green was their pastor. Young Oscar was in the reverend's confirmation class two years prior, and was confirmed by him into the Lutheran faith on May 10, 1874.

As Oscar sat with the men, he repeatedly stated how he wished they'd come by so he could use his father's "old gun" to help apprehend them. Oscar was instructed to help keep a lookout during the following days, and if he noticed anything suspicious to immediately alert the colonel.

Oscar would get his chance on the morning of September 21, 1874. According to the Watonwan County Historical Society: "as Oscar and his father were milking the cows two men walked by, bidding Oscar a civil good morning as they passed. Something in their appearance instantly convinced the boy that they were the bandits; and he ran to his father and said "There goes the robbers."" His father didn't believe him and instructed Oscar to go on with his work. The boy tried, but soon set down his milking pail and implored his father to let him take a horse to Madelia to notify the colonel. Oscar could see the four men as he spoke with his father. They were sitting under a tree, eating the breakfast given to them by Oscar's mother. His father eventually relented and Oscar was quickly off.

The tree where the Younger Brothers sat eating lunch and were spotted by Oscar Sorbel in 1876. Hanska, MN. Photo Credit: Author's Personal Collection.

From the Watonwan County Historical Society:

He instantly started for Madelia, seven or eight miles away, urging the old farm horse to the top of his speed, and shouting to everybody he passed, "Look out! The robbers are about!" but finding nobody to believe him. A short distance from Madelia the horse fell down, throwing the excited rider into the mud; but he was soon up and away again faster than ever. Entering Madelia, he rode straight to the Flanders House, according to his promise to Col. Vought. The latter was standing on the porch of the hotel when the messenger dashed up, boy and horse equally out of breath and both of them covered with mud.

Colonel Vought quickly formed a posse and set off in pursuit of the men. The Madelia Seven, as they'd later become known, spotted the gang on foot as they were crossing the Hanska Slough. The outlaws had been unsuccessful in stealing horses from a local farmer and were forced to evade on foot. The posse yelled for them to stop, but their command was ignored. The Madelia Seven then opened fire on the gang. The outlaws returned fire with their revolvers. The chase continued and the four men almost escaped by swimming through Lake Hanska, but they were soon apprehended. One of the gang, Charlie Pitts, was killed in the gunfire, but the three Younger Brothers were put in a wagon and taken the eight and a half miles back to Madelia to await their fate.

Word spread quickly. As they entered the town later that day the streets were lined with spectators. The Younger Brothers, wounded with multiple gunshots, waved their hats to the boisterous crowd as they were paraded down the main street.

The men were taken to Flanders House. Cole Younger greeted Colonel Vought with a salute and a greeting of "landlord" after Cole recognized the colonel from their stay earlier in the month. The hotel soon acted as both jail and hospital to the surviving men. They were fed, cleaned, and their wounds tended to.

Dozens of reporters, photographers, detectives, and townsfolk clamored to get a look at or a word with the bank robbers. One of their visitors was Oscar's mother, Guri Sorbel. Fearing retaliation by friends of the gang, she visited the prisoners with baskets of food. With tears in her eyes, she implored them to forgive her son. Two days later the brothers were moved to Faribault, Minnesota, in neighboring Rice County. They were placed in the county jail to await trail.

The apprehension of the Younger Brothers gang might have never happened if it weren't for the quick thinking of seventeen-year-old Oscar Sorbel. Reverend Green's farm was directly in the path of history. Young Oscar rode by Reverend Green's farm on his fervent errand to alert the Madelia posse. And after the apprehension, the posse, the badly wounded gang, and the body of Charlie Pitts rode again directly past the Green Farm on their way back to Madelia.

The Green Farm was two miles from the Flanders House hotel. Without a doubt Reverend Green knew of the harrowing event and of the captives being held down the road. It's even possible that he gave spiritual care to the three outlaw brothers. In another ironic connection, when Jesse and Frank James and James Younger were scoping out the area in August of 1876, they passed through Wanamingo Township. They stopped at the farm of Lars Gjemse for a meal, rest, and grain for their horses. The Gjemse Family were Norwegian immigrants who attended Wanamingo Lutheran Church, where Reverend Green had received his first call seven years prior. The two Larses knew each other well.

The Younger Brothers Capture Site Monument, LaSalle, MN.
Photo Credit: Author's Personal Collection.

That extremely painful year of 1876 was brightened early the following year when Lars and Jensine's fifth child, and first son, was born. Joseph Marinus Green was born on February 17, 1877, and baptized at Trinity Lutheran Church by his father. Jennie had been pregnant with him when she lost baby Lena Eliza, and when the Younger Brothers gang was captured a few miles from their home.

The Norwegian settlers in America brought with them a unique child naming custom. When a child died, it was common for the parents to name the next child of the same gender after the precious child who had been lost. The Green family followed this tradition. On May 15, 1878, their sixth child arrived, and they named her Marie Josephine Green, after her departed sister.

The first of Reverend Green's family members who emigrated from Norway to join him in southern Minnesota was his fourteen-year-old niece, Gina, who arrived in the spring of 1880. Gina's father, Bernt, was Reverend Green's older brother. Bernt lost his wife in December of 1879 when she was forty-seven-years old. Her death left her five children without a mother. After she passed, all the children, with the exception of her youngest son who was only ten years old at the time of her passing, eventually ended up leaving home for a new life in Minnesota. Gina was the first to leave for America.

Six months after her mother's passing, Gina Birgitte was almost fifteen-years-old when she appeared in the June 1880 U.S. Census. She is listed as "niece," living in the Green household in Madelia. It's difficult to imagine the strength and bravery it took for a fourteen-year-old to cross the ocean alone, and travel by boat and train across the country to waiting family with no way to seek help or resources if needed. Gina's arrival to the household was a welcome help to Jensine. She stayed with the family for approximately five years before moving north to Wisconsin.

The Hard Winter of 1880–1881 refers to the historically long, cold, and snowy winter across the central Great Plains. Winter arrived powerfully, unexpectedly, and far too early that year when a blizzard struck southern Minnesota on October 15, 1880, causing ten to twelve-foot drifts. Ponds froze, young calves died from the freezing temperatures, and potatoes froze in the ground, making them worthless.

On November 4, another blizzard hit. *The New Ulm Journal* reported on the politics of the day, with Garfield winning the presidency; local disease outbreaks of scarlet fever, tuberculosis and diphtheria; and the cold temperatures. It reported on thieves stealing wood from woodpiles, and a herd of cattle that drowned after they were driven into Lake Hanska by the most recent storm.

The bitter cold continued throughout November. In neighboring Renville County, when the people of Bird Island began to run out of wood, they took the wood reserved for the train engines. Throughout the entire area, all of the available grain had been threshed, and very little remained within most of the townships. A great deal of wheat and corn, unable to be harvested, was left to rot in the fields due to winter arriving so early and unexpectedly.

Yet another blizzard struck a month later on December 4. After this storm, residents began to take apart railroad bridges to use for heat in their stoves. In mid-December there was a lull in the storms, and the people took advantage of the nicer weather. With Christmas soon arriving, they headed to town for supplies and shopping. A passenger train carrying hundreds of passengers heading east derailed near Courtland. Several cars turned on their sides, and several others jumped the track. Cheyenne chiefs were on the train that day, and one reportedly said he "hated these new ways of travel." In New Ulm, a worker on the Redstone Railroad Bridge was swept off by the plow of a passing locomotive. He fell twenty feet into the snow bank below, but thankfully survived. Nearby counties reported a handful of people who had gotten lost and had frozen to death in the cold.

Fuel shortages continued. Many people switched to coal-burning stoves. Angry New Ulm residents watched as railroad cars full of wood passed by, headed towards eastern prairie towns in need of it. Another blizzard struck the day after Christmas, followed by another snowstorm just three days later on December 29. These back-to-back storms completely shut down rail service west of St. Peter for one week.

It was during this same week when a tragedy struck the Green Family once again. Reverend Green and Jensine's beloved six-year-old daughter Valborg died of diphtheria on December 31, 1880. The outbreak had taken dozens of other lives as well. Children were especially susceptible to the terrible sickness which inflamed the throat so badly that it blocked airways, making it impossible to breathe. Once again, the reverend, while grieving tremendously, performed the funeral and burial rites for his own child. Because public funerals were forbidden due to the epidemic, the reverend and Jennie quietly laid their daughter to rest on a frozen January day at Linden Lutheran Cemetery.

The massive fuel shortage continued into the New Year. Wood was scarce and susceptible to theft. Farmers began burning hay to survive. People were unable to bury their loved ones who had passed for two or three weeks due to the storms. The bodies of the deceased remained in coffins buried in snow at home before a trip to the cemetery could be made.

Another snowstorm hit on January 12 and 13. It took several days for tracks to be cleared for the trains. One hundred and fifty residents of Sleepy Eye and ninety residents of New Ulm shoveled tracks, only to have their work disappear with the next storm on January 30. The wind kept drifting the snow despite their constant shoveling.

Reverend Green almost lost his own life during the Hard Winter. In his memoir letter he described the frightening ordeal he lived through after making a sick call to Lake Hanska. While visiting an ill man, eight miles from the Green's home, a snowstorm began, and the man begged the reverend to stay the night. In the morning, the snow was so deep and the wind so fierce that he ended up staying with the sick man for three days.

Knowing Jennie and the children were at home worried about him, Reverend Green decided to gather his team and head for home the following morning. He was grateful to have his heavy fur coat and sturdy boots for the journey. Soon after setting off towards home, the horses kept falling through the snow drifts, and he realized they could not make the journey. He stopped at the Afdem Farm to stable his horses before heading back out on foot. He continued on until he came to the Harmandsen Farm, where he stopped to rest and warm himself for a while. The Harmandsens begged him to stay, but he insisted on resuming his trek towards home.

The snowfall continued and soon made walking impossible. As he passed by Gove Lake his boots kept filling with heavy snow and he couldn't move forward. It began to get dark, as the reverend became extremely cold and tired. He hadn't eaten anything in a while and was becoming weak from the exertion. Seeing an old oak tree ahead, he made his way towards it. He climbed the tree and sat on a heavy branch to catch his breath. He prayed for God to protect his family and to help him arrive home safely.

A few moments later, he heard a rooster crow. Knowing he was near a farm he climbed down and followed the sound of the rooster. The farm belonged to an American, who greeted him warmly and gave him tea to drink and warm stockings for his feet. After a brief rest, Reverend Green realized he was very close to home, only a few farms away, and so pushed on and made it home safely that night. His family was overjoyed to see him. He was unable to retrieve his team for ten more days due to the snow.

The worst storm that had ever been seen came on February 4, and lasted through the sixth. Snow drifts were between ten and twelve feet high. Shops were short on oil, coffee, and sugar, and all schools were closed. Because trains couldn't get through, horse-and-sleigh teams were hired to transport passengers to their destinations.

By mid-February of 1881, temperatures were fifteen degrees below zero, with no signs of letting up. Businesses in town struggled to keep their storefronts clear of snow, and one creative saloon served drinks to its customers from within a shoveled-out snowdrift. Farmers were forced to burn their wheat stores that had been reserved for spring planting. After two weeks, a train was finally able to get through, but on February 22 there was yet another storm. Passengers on two trains traveling through New Ulm were trapped for seven days. They survived by townspeople bringing them food and provisions.

In March of 1881, the snow was still deep in every direction. Cattle began to starve. Schools remained cancelled, and the newspapers stopped printing as well. People burned what they could, including furniture and corn cobs. There were rumors of farmers burning their plows and farm equipment, but the papers concluded those rumors were unfounded.

Snow blockade, Southern Minnesota. Chicago, Milwaukee and Saint Paul Railway. Original Image from the Minnesota Historical Society. Photo Credit: Elmer and Tenney. Public Domain

Through it all, the people still managed to attend dances and social events. The hopes of spring soon arriving were dashed when back-to-back storms continued on March 11 and 12, and again on the fourteenth and fifteenth. A woman was killed by a train that didn't see her walking along the tracks. On March 24, the first train since January was able to get through to Bird Island, and by the end of March there was finally some good news.

Enough snow had melted that wagons could finally be used instead of sleighs. Geese started to return. The people began to feel relieved, and hopeful that the storms were finally over, but much to their dismay another one arrived on March 30. By April 6, the ice on the Minnesota River was still thirty-six inches thick. Ultimately, the final blizzard of the long, cold winter occurred on April 10, once again blocking trains and making roads impossible to navigate.

On April 20, Reverend Green's fortieth birthday, the snow stopped, and the first rain of the season fell. After six months of brutal snow and freezing temperatures, winter was finally over, and spring had arrived. It was three days after Easter—a renewal of life had come to the land. The Native Americans had warned that a huge flood would soon be coming, as the ice began to thaw on the Minnesota River. This tremendous amount of melting snow and ice along the Great Plains was historic. The warning of the Native Americans proved to be correct when the Great Flood of 1881 caused significant damage throughout the Midwest. Locally, the Minnesota and Cottonwood Rivers flooded significantly, but thankfully the area served by Reverend Green was, for the most part, undamaged.

After the many terrible losses within his family that difficult year, the reverend prayed that the remainder of 1881 would be a year of peace—for his family, for his congregants, and for his community. As spring emerged, the snow thawed upon the roads leaving puddles and mud in its stead, and the first new buds could be seen on the linden trees. That year would prove to be historically significant for both Reverend Green and the people of Brown, Watonwan, and Blue Earth counties.

After the loss of three daughters within four years, the spring of 1881 brought a joyous breath of fresh air to the family. Ten members of his family arrived from Norway to join him in the Hanska area. His sisters Karen and Olava, his brother Gustav, Gustav's wife and five children, and his twenty-year-old nephew Axel left Norway together on March 30, 1881, aboard the SS *Angelo*. The steamer took two days to arrive in Hull, England, where the family then boarded a train for a three-hour ride to Liverpool. After a weeklong stay, they boarded another steamer, the SS *Bothnia*, on April 9, 1881, for the trans-Atlantic journey to America.

The Green family's voyage took twenty days from leaving the shores of Norway to arriving in New York Harbor. It was as if the hand of God was safely guiding them to their beloved brother and uncle, because the day they arrived was a particularly special one. The ten weary passengers first set foot upon American soil on Reverend Green's fortieth birthday, April 20, 1881. From New York, the family took a smaller steamer up the Hudson River and Erie Canal. The steamer then crossed the Great Lakes into La Cross, Wisconsin. From there they took a train to Minneapolis, and then switched trains to New Ulm, likely arriving in mid-May of 1881. The railroad had yet to reach Hanska or Madelia, but Reverend Green brought extra wagons with him to New Ulm and greeted his weary family on that joyous spring day. Much exciting news of home was shared during the wagon ride back to Madelia.

Lars Green hadn't seen his three siblings in fifteen years. On the day they arrived, he met his brother Gustav's children for the very first time. He hadn't seen his nephew Axel since he was a five-year-old boy back home in Norway. Axel was only a small child when his uncle left, but was now a grown man. Room was made at the Green farm to accommodate all the new arrivals.

Many in Norway had received letters from family and friends who had immigrated to the Midwest of America describing tornadoes. Stories were written describing the terror and fury of winds so powerful they could obliterate an entire farm and homestead within seconds. The horror was heightened by descriptions of tornadoes descending with little warning, indiscriminately decimating one farm while sparing neighbors on every side. Gustav had heard these tales, and after only being in Hanska for three months, he would become witness to one of the most catastrophic tornadoes Minnesota had ever seen.

It was a hot, clear summer day on Friday, July 15, 1881. The extended Green family were hurrying to finish their afternoon work when the skies started to change and turn dark. They had been planning to celebrate Gustav's thirty-fifth birthday that evening, his first in America.

The Greens had another reason to celebrate that day. Gustav had achieved his American Dream and had proudly purchased his homestead in Hanska only two weeks prior. Gustav claimed an eighty-acre homestead and moved his large family out of his brother's barn and onto their own property.

By 4 p.m. that afternoon, it was clear there would be no celebrating. A cluster of six tornadoes tormented southern Minnesota that afternoon, the worst of which was an F4 that created a forty-mile path of destruction, obliterating everything in its track. The mighty wind saved its most deadly devastation for the town at the end of the forty-mile stretch before it dissipated over the Minnesota River. The town at the tail end of the tornado's fury was New Ulm.

The following description is from the July 20 edition of the *New Ulm Review*:

Our city was visited on Friday July 15 by one of the most terrific cyclones ever witnessed in the State of Minnesota.

The day was extremely warm, the mercury standing at 90 degrees in the shade, at noon and the gentle southerly breeze afforded but slight relief from the oppressive heat. At half past three o'clock in the afternoon, the low roll of thunder called the attention of our citizens to a heavy, black cloud in the north western horizon, and fifteen minutes later another was seen rising from the South-west. These two advancing columns seemed to intersect each other, 30 degrees west of the zenith, and the united column moved onward toward the east in rapid, spiral curves, while the deep hazen color of the cloud within the western angle of these two columns, the terrific peals of thunder and incessant flashes of lightening gave ominous forebodings of the power of the demon of destruction who was threatening to hurl his tempests upon us. Windows were hastily closed and awnings furled, and at fifteen minutes past four, the storm came in all its fury, and no pen can describe the scene that followed.

The fist gust destroyed nearly every chimney in the city. Next tin roofs were stripped off and blown in every direction, and crumbled into every conceivable shape; doors, windows, boards, shingles, rafters, bricks and branches of trees were seen flying through the air in every direction; whole roofs were torn off and came crashing into the sides of buildings on the opposite side of the street as if hurled by the power of Milton's demons; buildings were lifted from their foundations and scattered and twisted into shapeless masses of ruins; massive brick buildings trembled and crumbled before the blast as if shaken by an earthquake.

During all this destruction the fearful shriek of the tempest the perpetual roar of the thunder, the crash of falling walls mingled with the screams of terrified men, women and children rendered the scene one that beggars all description and baffles all language.

The city, after the tempest had passed, presented a scene of sadness never to be forgotten by those who witnessed it. The debris of the fallen buildings, wagons, farm-machinery, furniture and clothing were mingled in one promiscuous mass from one end of the city to the other; trees were stripped of their branches, and twisted and knotted as if by the hand of a giant; horses, some dead and others still struggling, were buried beneath the timbers of fallen stables; mothers were searching and anxiously inquiring for missing children; and the bewildered and terror-stricken people were standing and gazing in sad silence upon all that remained of their ruined homes. The storm only lasted about 15 minutes, but in that brief time the destruction of property and life was great.

The people however were not long in recovering their equilibrium, and the good work of relief to the maimed and wounded was at once begun. Drs Berry, Muller and Carl assisted by Dr. Oldberg of St. Paul, who was in New Ulm on a visit, and the Sisters of Charity done all in their power to relief the poor victims of the terrible tempest, and before darkness had set in nearly or quite every person wounded had been taken care of. The first effects of the tornado were felt in the northern part of the town, among the modest residences of the laboring portion of the community. These were somewhat scattered, but within less than two minutes were all either carried off bodily or leveled to the ground. Over a hundred dwellings, all of modest pretentions, were absolutely swept away on the wings of the wind, and several hundred people rendered homeless and penniless. Furniture, clothing, and bedding was carried away in the general destruction, and very many saved nothing except the clothing they had on at the time. Trees and vegetation were razed even with the earth. Minn. Street and Broadway the two principal thoroughfares were blocked by the debris of the destroyed buildings.

The article goes on to describe in detail the list and manner of deaths, injuries, and loss of property and livestock. It tells of both people and animals lifted into the air and carried for nearly a mile, and heavy chunks of iron and timber found deeply embedded into the ground. A newborn was found among the living, the only survivor of her large family, and a horse was found alive and unharmed in a tree. Half of New Ulm was obliterated. Many prayers of thanks were given by the Norwegian communities of Hanska, Linden, Butternut, and Madelia who were spared from the cyclone's devastation. Everyone in the neighboring communities did what they could to assist their New Ulm neighbors.

The summer of 1881 was also a spiritually difficult one for Reverend Green. There was discontent amongst some of his parishioners in the Lake Hanska Lutheran congregation. A few years earlier in 1879, a few of them had walked eight miles to Madelia to hear a lecture by Kristofer Janson. Janson, a good friend of the famous playwright Henrik Ibsen, was a poet and author from Norway on a lecturing tour. He held a degree in theology from the University of Christiana, but his speeches condemned church hierarchy and questioned doctrine, making him very unpopular with the Church of Norway. Janson was convinced there might be an audience for his teachings amongst the Norwegian immigrants in America, so he moved to Minneapolis and officially became a Unitarian minister.

A group of Reverend Green's congregants at Lake Hanska Lutheran were so taken by Janson's teachings that they began to question their place within the Lutheran church. They considered their ideology and if it belonged elsewhere. Several of them decided it was time for a final split from Reverend Green's congregation. They officially left the church and formed a Unitarian Universalist church in Hanska. Questions regarding church control, predestination, slavery, the role of public verses private schooling, and the burying on church grounds the parishioners who died by suicide were some of the differences.

65

It was undoubtedly very painful for the reverend to have these discussions with his parishioners, and to try and hold his flock together. These were people he knew well and loved like family. He'd presided over their marriages, confirmations, and baptisms. He was with them through all walks of their life, both joyous and sorrowful. It wounded him deeply knowing they wanted to leave the church—and in his mind, eternal salvation.

The newly formed Unitarian church asked Kristofer Janson if he'd consider becoming their minister. He agreed to spend the summer months preaching in Hanska, and the rest of the year preaching to his Minneapolis congregation. In August of 1881, the Nora Unitarian Universalist Congregation of Hanska was officially organized. It was named "Nora" for "Norwegian."

On the day the new church was dedicated, Kristofer Janson stood atop Mount Pisquah high on the church's property and raised the Norwegian flag. Teams of wagons came from all directions, until the congregation numbered around four hundred people. Reverend Green was saddened to lose them, but the first members of the new church rejoiced in finding a house of worship they wholly identified with, though it came at a cost.

Over the years, the congregation was bitterly assailed, not only by its neighbors, but in the Norwegian press…They were barraged with slander and abuse from every side, even from the local pulpits. It was extremely difficult for these liberal pioneers, for they no longer had the support of the Norwegian church and all the tradition that went with that, or of a resident pastor to lead them and care for their needs…It was very lonely. People who had come from the same town in Norway and been friends for years no longer spoke to the Unitarians. All of the support provided by the Norwegian church to the immigrants was unavailable to the members of Nora church. — Nora Unitarian Universalist Church www.norauuchurch.org

Nora Unitarian Universalist Church was built on a Native American burial ground. Named Mount Pisquah by the early Jesuit priests in the area, the hill on the church property is the highest point in Brown County. When the foundation was being dug, several Native American bones were discovered, each sitting atop their own boulder in a ceremonial display. The skeletons were reburied on the property.

On July 21, 1883, after two years of hard work and waiting, the official church building was nearly completed. It had been almost two years to the day since the deadly F4 tornado leveled New Ulm when another tornado struck the area. The tornado again struck Brown County, but this time it hit "Little Norway," Hanska.

Reverend Janson was in the newly completed church with his family and the carpenters when it was blown apart by a tornado. The sixteen people went flying, sliding down the hill into the woods below and barely making it out alive. Janson lost his new church, his summer home, and all of his written books including his new manuscript. All of the money he'd collected was flown throughout the county, most of which was found, and returned, by the citizens.

*The local Lutherans declared that God had spoken against the heresy of these liberals, even though the same tornado also put the Lake Hanska church askew on its foundation. — Nora Unitarian Universalist Church.*www.norauuchurch.org

Kristofer Janson wrote many of his best novels and poems during his summers on the beautiful hill of Nora Church where he was pastor for twelve years. In 1893, he returned to Norway to introduce Unitarianism to his home country. He is not only the founder of Nora Unitarian Universalist Church in tiny Hanska, but he is the founder of the entire Norwegian Unitarian Church. Reverends Janson and Green knew each other. Janson wrote and spoke openly about his disdain for the Norwegian Evangelical Lutheran Church of America—the synod that Reverend Green belonged to.

It would be nice to imagine the two men cordially tipping their hats to one another as their buggies passed on the dirt roads of Brown County. It would be nice to imagine the two Norwegian immigrant pastors uniting in civility for the common good of their community brethren, but in reality, there was likely much strain between the two.

Nora Unitarian Universalist Church. Hanska, MN. Photo Credit: Gil Hanson.

Reverend Green's oldest daughter Annie was twelve years old, his son Joseph five, and his youngest daughter Marie four when the family welcomed another daughter on January 15, 1882. The baby girl shared her birthday with her Aunt Karen, Lars' sister, who had arrived to Hanska less a year earlier. She was the seventh child born to Lars and Jensine—a girl they named Valborg Wilhelmine. She was named after her departed sister, who had died of diphtheria twelve months earlier during the Hard Winter.

The next decade of Reverend Green's life was spent tending to the spiritual needs of his local congregations within Brown, Watonwan, and Blue Earth Counties. He continued to perform marriages, baptisms, and burials for both community members and his own relatives. Gustav and Andrea welcomed their first daughter, Sigri Amelia, in August 1882, and she was baptized by her uncle on August 20 at Lake Hanska Lutheran.

Sadly however, the baby would only live for one month after her baptism. She died September 20. The following fall on October 3,

Gustav tragically lost his wife Andrea on the same day she gave birth to their second daughter, Gina Amalie.

On March 29, 1883, Reverend Green officiated the wedding of his sister Karen to Ellef Asleson at Trinity Lutheran in Madelia. Ellef was a widower, and had been caring for his three small children since his first wife died the previous year. Once married, Karen became a loving mother to Ellef's three young children. The couple never had children of their own. Karen lived in Linden, on the family farm, until her passing in 1934.

Jethro, the father-in-law of Moses, was famous for his seven daughters. Like the Biblical patriarch, Reverend Green welcomed his seventh daughter to the world on March 20, 1884. Lars and Jensine were both forty-three years old when she was born. Nellie Elise was baptized by her father during the Easter Sunday service at Trinity Lutheran in Madelia. She was the last child born to the couple, and sadly, she was also the last child the loving couple would bury.

Baby Nellie died at home on the family farm on September 15, 1884, from "summer complaint" according to county records. She was only six months old. Nellie's gravestone is incorrectly marked 1882 instead of 1884, the true year of her short life. Of Lars and Jensine's eight children, only four survived to adulthood. At Trinity Lutheran Cemetery, the four little girls who were lost are laid beside each other in a single heartbreaking row.

Five days after baby Nellie died, the cruel hand of fate touched Gustav once again on September 20. His baby daughter Gina Amalie, whose mother Andrea died during her delivery, became sick a few weeks shy of her first birthday and died as well. That terrible day was also the second anniversary of Gustav's daughter Sigri's passing.

As Reverend Green treaded the dark waters of his own grief, he provided spiritual comfort to his grieving brother as well. The two brothers were a solace to each other and leaned on one another in the shared, unimaginable pain of losing their babies only days apart.

For Lake Hanska Lutheran Church's eighty-fifth anniversary in 1954, church member Petra Lien Molmen submitted the following article describing what Christmastime was like for the Norwegian Lutherans of the prairie, with Reverend Green as minister, as remembered by her elderly aunt.

Church Services When Tante Kristianne Lien Was Young

The children too considered church attendance a great privilege in spite of long sermons. It was not every day or every week that children could go somewheres. In the 1880s services were held only once every four weeks because "Kab" could only make one church a Sunday. From his home north of Madelia to Lake Hanska was eight miles.

The whole family came to church, including the wee babies. Nobody minded them because a number of them were customarily in church, and customarily a few of them cried during services. You couldn't much blame them when you remember the blankets, and blankets and some more blankets that they were wrapped in. Later the "skrikar rum" or baby crying room was built on at the south east corner of the church; and the sacristy was built on the south west corner for the minister.

Tante tells how cold the benches were after not being heated for four weeks. There was a black stove shaped like a drum standing in the middle of the church, and rods and rods of black stove pipes. Whole logs were put in at a time. She remembers yet the fascination of watching the heat rings in that cold air.

Foot warmers had not yet come into use. A foot warmer was a sort of drawer inside of a carpet covered metal container into which we put burning pieces of charcoal. It seems we used them as late as 1910.
For myself I remember Jakob Bakke as "klokker" and I wish we still had him. I also remember Toline Bakke as organist. Tante remembers Bargoust and how he helped Reverend Green into his ministerial gown and ceremoniously tied the fluted collar around his

70

neck before services. Our church had no sacristy then so this performance was by the alter, in full sight of the congregation.

Then he clearly read the opening prayer: Lord we enter now into this Holy House, to hear what Thou, O Lord would have us believe and do: His light blue eyes gazed heavenward. Throughout the service he stood at attention and in his strong voice gave a very sanctimonious "Amen" to all ministerial rites. To people of that age baptisms, for instance, would not seem nearly so holy without those "Amens."

All babies were baptized in church. In the case of illness or something radically wrong, the whole neighborhood was concerned if a baby was baptized at home.

At any church service there was always a long row of women carrying babies for baptism. All mothers carrying boys were first in line, then came those who carried girls.

Bergoust stood at the front of the church, and clearly in a strong voice led the singing. He also led a choir and taught parochial school.

For these services he collected a bushel of wheat from each farmer. Tante still remembers how he came driving into the yard with his little wagon. Collecting wasn't always easy, especially when times were hard. One farmer, for instance, told him he could very well sing without a "klokker."

All the men sat on the west side of the church and all the women on the east side. People did a little whispered gossiping about the first women who had the audacity to sit on the men's side. They were considered slightly "fresh" such as women who bobbed their hair in 1915 or 1920.

Everybody looked forward to Christmas. Somehow even children realized that the coming of the Christ-child and His sacrificial love for mankind was the event that gave security to life.

71

Mortgaged property or anything else might be taken away, but never the happiness of Christmas.

Weeks ahead we planned. Weeks ahead we gladly at many a meal of clabbered milk and mush for there was joy and pride in feeding guests sumptuously at Christmas.

Evidently, in olden times Norway Christmas wasn't really over until the twentieth day but in our community where lack of opportunity and determination to get an education made it necessary for young folks to go away from home, perhaps for eighth grade, High school or College Education. I think people thought of Christmas lasting the two weeks the children were home for vacation.

Christmas eve, the twenty-fourth was always the family Christmas eve. Then father read the second chapter of Luke, our family sang all the Christmas songs we knew, we children spoke the "pieces" we had learned for the school and church programs. We admired our Christmas tree. It wasn't always an evergreen. Money couldn't be spent carelessly when you were knee deep in debts at 6% or 8% or even 10% interest. But it was ours and we had learned at school how to make clever trimmings from popcorn, pieces of straw from the straw pile and bits of colored paper from the Sears Roebuck catalog, also cranberries. That was the evening when people in our community opened their gifts, usually useful ones like mittens, stockings, etc.

My grandmother from Madelia, the Liens from Hanska, and the Slettas were there so we were a happy family.

Christmas day was reserved for church. Chores and twice to church was all there was time for that day. How festive that always was! Even people who didn't come to church the rest of the year came that day and the church was always packed. Then there was the Christmas tree festival in the evening consisting of recitations and songs by the children of the congregation. Always there was lots of treats for the children and gifts passed around.

*Second day Christmas the dinner parties started and we were
some place or else had company every day or evening until after New
Years. That was the era when neighbors were neighbors and really
felt like one family. As a child I think there were few homes in all Lake
Hanska where we hadn't been guests.*

*Prior to 1915 we had a surrey (carriage), but for Christmas
time travelling the old bob sled was really it. Father had straw in the
bottom of it, then we laid quilts and "skinfeller," Norwegian sheep
skin robes on top of the straw, then we had some more of them to put
on top of us. Sometimes there were so many clothes that we got stiff
from sitting there. But even our faces could be tucked underneath if
the weather bit too hard. Father had to sit on the wagon seat at front
to drive the horses and got the worst of the weather. But he had a big
dog skin coat brought from Norway and he had a robe over his knees
made of horseshide. Sometimes the road was bare in spots and we had
to drive in the ditch, as the sled runner wouldn't slide. Lots of times
young folks had lots of fun spilling whole sledfuls of people that way.*

*Sometimes the trip took us several hours for we went to these
dinner parties at Ole K. Brostes, Fredericksons, Amundsons,
Frederick Jorgensons, Marin Paulsons, as well as all our nearby
neighbors.*

*Then sometimes we children would say, Today let's lay the
reins down and see where the horses go. Not guided they would go to
Slettas, where Morton Jacobson now lives.*

*Turns in the road had to be made differently with horses than
with cars but those horses knew how to make them just right. And of
course if we met anyone on the road they always stopped. All horses
at that time expected people to visit a while with anyone they met on
the road.*

*Many people in the community had sleighbells. It was sort of
an introduction to a happy party when beautiful, well-kept horses
came prancing up to a farmyard with the sleighbells jingling. How
majestic they seemed.*

But don't think that these Christmas parties didn't mean weeks of preparation. No stores had Ready mixes. I don't remember making lutefisk. We always bought it. But mother often told about Grandma. Grandpa cut nice clean pieces of oak. Grandma scrubbed the inside of the stove then burned the oak wood until she had clean white ashes. These she put in a huge crock and poured water over them. This mixture then stood for a week before she drained the liquid off. This had turned into lye water. Into this she put big hard pieces, four feet long of dried cod-fish which she had soaked in water for several days. Then that mixture had to sit another three weeks before it was similar to the lutefisk we eat today.

It was a long process but traditional for Christmas eve was rice soup cooked in milk, lutefisk rolled in lefse with lots of butter, spareribs, potatoes, etc.

Molasses "øl" was commonly made. It was nice to serve guests with kringla, berline kranser, føttigman, or Christmas cake with citron in. Even people who came on errands had to have something to eat or else according to tradition they would take the Joy of Christmas away from the house.

Then before Christmas there was butchering making of head cheese, rulle pølse and all the rest – all the bread-baking, crocks full of doughnuts, etc. etc. etc. Well-fed people were jovial visitors.

Children on a pony-drawn sled. 1909. Photo Credit: Library of Congress. Public Domain.

Reverend Green's brother Gustav decided to return to Norway in the winter of 1885, after the tragic loss of his second wife Andrea and their two young daughters. In preparation for his journey, he sold his homestead to his and Lars' sister Karen and her husband Ellef Asleson in November directly before leaving the country. With the exception of his five-year-old son Karl, whom he brought with him back to Norway, Gustav's three sons from his first wife were sent to live and work on local farms when he departed. Reverend Green was a positive paternal influence to his teenage nephews during their father's absence.

As the terribly painful decade of the 1880s came to a close, and the twentieth century neared, life for the Norwegian Lutheran community started to get a little easier. The 1890s were a decade of relative peace for the Green family. Gustav did not stay in Norway; he returned to Hanska in 1893 along with Karl, a new wife, and four new children. The 1895 Minnesota Census lists the family as farming in Hanska. He was renting farmland that was once his, but now belonged to his sister and her husband. Shortly after the census, he moved his family north to Greenbush, in Roseau County, where Gustav remained for the rest of his life. He wanted to own his own land once again.

With the coming of the new century, Reverend Green began to contemplate his retirement and how he wanted to spend his remaining years. After decades of faithful service to his community, he began the bittersweet process of passing his four beloved congregations down to the next generation of clergymen. His departure from the ministry was not sudden, but would occur gradually over another decade.

The Sunset

The Green Family. L-R, Annie, Rev. Lars, Valborg, Jensine, Joseph, Marie.
Photo Credit: Friends of Linden Lutheran Church

*T*he year 1900 arrived, and with it the promise of a new, modern era. Even though Reverend Green was nearing retirement from his official duties, his love and commitment to his family and community continued to be as strong as ever, long into and after he formally retired. His venerable career as the tireless minister to the four-point "Green Parish" of Lake Hanska, Linden, Madelia, and Butternut started to shift direction around the turn of the twentieth century.

Reverend Green continued to preach his sermons at his four churches, to baptize babies, bury beloved community members, and officiate over many weddings as the new century dawned. Three of those weddings were of his nephews—Gustav's sons who arrived from Norway in 1881 as young children, who were left to fend for themselves as teenage farmhands when their father returned to

Norway for seven years, and who all remained in the area as young men when he moved to northern Minnesota.

Reverend Green's nephew Frithjof was married at Trinity Lutheran Church on June 6, 1900. Frithjof's brother Bernhard wed later that same month on June 29, at Linden Lutheran. His third nephew Olaf asked his Uncle Lars to officiate his wedding as well, two years later on October 29, 1902, at Trinity Lutheran. The reverend would also perform the baptisms for Olaf's four children and Bernhard's two daughters at Lake Hanska Lutheran. Gustav's other two children by his first wife, Clara and Karl, were both married by a Justice of the Peace in New Ulm. Clara's daughter, Gunda, had been baptized by her great-uncle at Lake Hanska Church on New Year's Day, 1886.

As he approached his sixtieth decade, the reverend decided that being the pastor of four congregations was becoming too much for him. He realized it was time for a change. The first congregation he said farewell to, passing the pulpit to the next generation, was Lake Hanska Lutheran in 1900—also the same year the church left the four-point parish. It's not known why Reverend Green chose to leave Lake Hanska at that time when he didn't leave the others for another seven to eight years.

The successor to Lake Hanska's pulpit was Reverend Gregor Olsen Skaret, who served from 1900 to 1906. Reverend Skaret was followed by Reverend H. Hvid who served a brief term from 1906–1907, before he was replaced by Reverend J. M. Nergiv from 1907–1910.

On June 2, 1901, Reverend Green led the dedication ceremony of the newly formed First Lutheran Church in Butterfield, Minnesota, outside of St. James in southern Watonwan County. The new church building was twenty-six feet wide, forty feet long, and fourteen feet high, with an entry ten-by-ten feet. Twenty benches and two Rochester Lamps were purchased for the new congregation.

The first Ladies' Aid group of Zion Lutheran Church was organized in 1901. Two years later, in November 1903, Reverend

Skaret, then pastor of Lake Hanska Lutheran, first formulated the idea of starting a church in the town. As the children of the pioneers were coming of age and starting their own families, the village of Hanska was being expanded. New homes and shops were being built, and it seemed only fitting that a church and school be included as well.

Thirteen families, the ones who lived closer to the newly developed town, originally branched off from Lake Hanska Lutheran to form Zion Lutheran. The name they first decided upon was "Zion's Scandinavian Lutheran Church," but it was later simplified. The first services were held in the upstairs of Nundahl's Hall, which later became The Muni bar and restaurant, a town icon for decades.

Once spring arrived in 1904, the digging of the foundation began for the new church. With no modern equipment, the men used only shovels and wheelbarrows. The foundation itself was made of stones hauled by horse and wagon from local farms.

On Tuesday afternoon, June 6, 1904, all places of business in Hanska were closed for the laying of the corner stone. The Cornerstone was purchased in Kasota, Minnesota, for $7.00. Presiding at the cornerstone laying service was Reverend Jens Mathieson of St. James. Reverend Green gave the prayer and invocation, and the sermon itself was delivered by Reverend L. P. Thorkveen of Albin. The prayers, invocation, and sermon were all held in Norwegian. English wouldn't be used during church services until decades later.

The church members had the foresight to place a sealed tin box of their current artifacts underneath the cornerstone. The contents of this time capsule included a history of the Zion Lutheran Church, a copy of the *Hanska Herald*, the *Madelia Times Messenger*, and *The New Voice*, as well as the following Norwegian publications: *Skandinavn, Decorah Posten, Ungdommen's Ven, Gammel og Ung, Sondags Skol Blad, Luteranen.*

In the summer of 1904, Reverend Green decided that he wasn't getting any younger, and if he wanted to see Norway again the time had come. He officially took a year-long leave of absence from

Linden Lutheran on September 25, and began planning for a solo trip back to the country of his birth. As plans were being made for the journey, his son Joseph was married in Decorah, Iowa, on June 15, 1905. Like Joseph, his wife Agnes Estrem was the daughter of Norwegian immigrants. It's unknown if the proud parents were able to make the 185-mile journey to attend the blessed event. Likely not, because Reverend Green completed the 1905 Minnesota State Census in Madelia the previous day on June 14.

The reverend's only son had followed in his father's footsteps. Prior to his marriage, he had become a Lutheran minister after graduating from St. Olaf College in Northfield, Minnesota, followed by Lutheran seminary in St. Paul.

The date Reverend Green left America for Europe in 1905 is unknown, but details of his return trip exist. He arrived to Grinkelsrud in the summer of 1905. It had been almost forty years since he'd seen his siblings, old friends, and childhood home. He would meet many new family members for the first time during that trip, including his brother Bernt's eight-year-old son, Guul*. Lars would not be able to reunite with his older brother Bernt however. He had passed away just a few months before Lars' arrival. Bernt had taken the last name "Green" in honor of Lars when he left to become a minister in America. Bernt was sixty-two years old when his son Guul was born. Young Guul met his Uncle Lars for the first, and only, time during that trip. One can imagine him sitting upon the floor of the main room as the adults gathered around to hear the many tales about life in America. Guul would hear about the adventures and lives of his older siblings whom he would never meet—Axel, Emma, Gina and Lars.

After a joyful reunion and visit, the day arrived when it was time once again to depart the shores of Norway. On September 27, 1905, Reverend Green said his final goodbyes to his dear family. He knew he would never see them again. Waving to him as he departed Oslo Harbor was his young nephew Guul.

*Guul is the great-grandfather of the author of this book.

The boy celebrated his ninth birthday that same day his Uncle Lars left Norway forever. It was likely a very emotional day for the reverend as the ship pulled away from the dock and he watched the land of the midnight sun slowly disappear into the horizon.

The ship that brought Reverend Green away from Norway's coast was the same ship that brought his brother, sisters, nieces and nephews to America a quarter of a century prior: the *SS Angelo*. The passenger list shows Lars Green, male, married, age sixty-four, destination: "Amerika."

This particular run would be one of the *Angelo*'s final voyages. According to the Norway Heritage website at www.norwayheritage.com: "On November 10th 1905, the *Angelo* departed from Christiania with emigrants for the last time. She had then done more than 700 voyages between Christiania and Hull, conveying the emigrants on their first stage on their way to America. In February 1906 she was sold to White & White for scrapping." She was decommissioned the following spring.

SS *Angelo* leaving Christiana, 1905.
Photo Credit: Library of Congress. Public Domain.

As Reverend Green's ship pulled into New York Harbor, he saw Lady Liberty for the very first time. The good reverend arrived at Ellis Island on Friday, October 13, 1905. On the passenger list he was described as "Scandinavian." His name and age were listed, as was his profession of "minister," and his ability to read and write. His purpose was listed as "Returning Home to Madelia, MN." And return he did, for the remainder of his life.

Shortly after he returned from Norway, Zion Lutheran, the new church in Hanska village for which Reverend Green had given the prayer and invocation at the cornerstone laying the previous year, was ready for its first sermon to its congregation. On a snowy Christmas morning of 1905, Zion Lutheran held its very first service in the newly built structure. Like the other surrounding churches, all the worship services were spoken in Norwegian. The first English services were offered in 1917, and those were only offered twice a year. Reverend Skaret, who took over Reverend Green's position at Lake Hanska, was Zion Lutheran's first pastor.

It's not known when Reverend Green retired as pastor of Our Saviour's Lutheran Church in Butternut Valley, but it was likely around the summer of 1906, when both Madelia and Butternut Valley congregations left the Linden Parish. The turn of the century brought several major changes to the area in terms of growth, population, technology, and culture. During this first decade of the twentieth century, there was much shifting of pastors and parishes. A new era of modern America had arrived as the pioneering days slowly slipped away.

The next congregation to say farewell to dear Reverend Green was Linden Lutheran Church in 1907. In June of that year, the church sent a call to Reverend J. M. Nervig, who accepted the role as their new pastor, ending the thirty-four years of service by Reverend Lars Green. The church's new pastor was installed on November 10, 1907, by Pastor Green. It was likely an emotional service for everyone as Reverend Green took off his robes for the last time and handed them to Reverend Nervig. Pastor Nervig was called to serve Lake Hanska, as well as Linden, and it was voted upon that he could also serve Zion Lutheran at his discretion as well.

The *Hanska Herald*, the newspaper of the tiny town where so many residents knew and loved Reverend Green, wrote an article about his retirement. Unfortunately, the specific date is unknown, but it was likely in November 1907, when he officially retired from Linden Lutheran.

Aged Pastor Retires:
Rev. L. E. Green Retires From Active and Successful Career

Rev. L. E. Green, pastor of the Norwegian Linden Lutheran church has retired from church work. On account of his constant and continued activity in religious circles and his advanced age he has found it necessary to retire from his life work. Rev. Green assumed the pastorship of the Linden congregation with which he has been constantly connected 33 years ago. He was a pioneer and a faithful worker. Like the congregation he has advanced in age, at the same time it has experienced a remarkable growth spiritually as well as physically. His predominating influence has been the means of keeping the body in harmonizing and friendly spirit. He has baptized 557 children, confirmed 414 people, married 89 couples, and solemnized 239 funerals.

Rev. Green delivered his farewell sermon last Sunday. Most all of the members were present and the church was filled to its utmost capacity. A feeling mingled with regret and pleasure is evident as Rev. Green severs his connection with the congregation. The many friends of Rev. Green wish him a long, pleasant, and prosperous future. — *Hanska Herald*, Date Unknown

Reverend Green gave a bittersweet farewell to the last of the four original parishes that he had led for decades—the last of the four-point Green Parish. He officially retired from Trinity Lutheran Church in Madelia in 1908. To this day, he holds the record as the longest serving pastor in the church's history. He likely stayed on with this congregation longer than the others due to its close proximity of less than two miles from his farm. As he entered retirement, the reverend remained a prominent presence within the Norwegian Lutheran communities of central-southern Minnesota.

On May 9, 1909, Reverend Green was invited to the fiftieth wedding anniversary of Gunder and Olia Paulson. The couple had wed in 1859, and were amongst the earliest Norwegian settlers of Brown County in the late 1850s. They were also among the earliest, founding members of Linden Lutheran Church.

Gunder, born on Christmas Day in 1825, lived a long life of eighty-eight years. He is laid to rest in the Linden Cemetery beside his beloved Olia, who died the year after their fiftieth anniversary celebration. Gunder and Olia's great-great grandson Randy Paulson is still very active on the board of the Friends of Linden Lutheran Church and Cemetery Association. Also currently on the board is Larry Harbo, the great-grandson of Jens and Secelia Harbo, whose cabin was the location of the founding of Linden Lutheran in 1859.

Another board member, Alan Thormodson, is the great-grandson of Peder Thormodson. Peder's farm was the location of the first Linden cemetery, before it was moved to its current location. Peder was one of the neighbors who found John Armstrong, who was killed during the Dakota War, and the one who extracted the arrow from his back.

Also active on the board is Joel Botten, whose family, the Omsrud-Thordsons, were one of the thirteen founding families of Linden Lutheran in 1859, as well as Lake Hanska Lutheran ten years later. Joel's great-great grandfather Thor Omsrud arrived by ox-driven covered wagon in 1857. The very first church services for Lake Hanska Lutheran were held under a big oak tree in a grove on their land.

Both Botten and Harbo are local historians whose knowledge of Linden–Hanska history and genealogy is extensive and deep. It can only be described as astonishing that the descendants of the first few Norwegian families to a desolate prairie land in the 1850s still gather as friends and family, working to keep the legacy of their forefathers and churches alive today.

Guul Green. 1947. Rolf's father. Author's Great-Grandfather.
Photo Credit: Author's Personal Collection.

May 9, 1909. Gunder and Olia Paulson 50th Wedding Anniversary. Linden, MN.
Photo Courtesy of Randy Paulson, Great-Great Grandson of Gunder and Olia
Paulson.

May 9, 1909. Rev. Lars E. Green and guests at Gunder and Olia Paulson 50th Wedding Anniversary. Linden, MN.
Photo Courtesy Of Randy Paulson, Great-Great Grandson of Gunder and Olia Paulson.

In 1910, Lake Hanska, Linden, and Zion Churches all found themselves without a pastor when Reverend Nervig resigned as minister. They knew the perfect man to help in their time of need. They called upon the good and faithful Reverend Green to fill in until a permanent replacement could be found. For one year, Reverend Green once again became their full-time minister. He was seventy years old and had three congregations to manage, but that was not a problem for the untiring reverend.

The following year, in November 1911, a permanent pastor was found, Reverend Carl Gustav Bjelland, who accepted the call to all three churches. He and his wife Minnie lived in the parsonage across the street from Lake Hanska, where the three youngest of their four children were born. Reverend Green's daughter, Marie, was the midwife who delivered the three babies of the pastor who replaced her father. The couple's first child Luther was born in 1914, followed by Lois in 1916, then Glendor in 1917. Reverend Bjelland served all three congregations from 1911 to 1920.

After the new pastor was found to relieve him, Reverend Green at last hung up his pastoral robes and walked away from the pulpit for the final time. After living on a farm for the entirety of his life, the reverend, along with Jensine, Annie, and Valborg moved to the big city of Minneapolis in 1912. Annie was forty-two and Valborg thirty years old.

Their new house at 3152 Elliot Avenue was built in 1908. With the sale of their Madelia farm, the family was able to purchase the home free and clear. The four-bedroom, one-bathroom, two-and-a-half-story house was almost 1,900 square feet. It was built in the simple American Foursquare architectural style. These "Prairie Box" homes were very common to Minnesota and the Midwest around the turn of the century. They were built to be a more practical and less ornate version of its cousin, the Victorian, while still taking pride in the interior wood craftsmanship. This was the final home Reverend Green would know.

The Green Family's new house was two and a half miles from Bethlehem Norwegian Lutheran Church, where they became active members and attended regularly. Like the Norwegian churches back home on the prairie, Bethlehem Lutheran's records were written in Norwegian, and the services conducted in Norwegian as well. One can envision the two elderly parents, arm-in-arm, strolling to church along the tree-lined sidewalk on sunny Sunday mornings. Reverend

Green had a cane in one hand and would tip his hat to passersby, his two daughters following behind.

The family's home was mere steps from Powderhorn Park, a sprawling sixty-five-acre recreational park built around Powderhorn Lake in the 1880s. Back in Reverend Green's time, the neighborhood was a beautiful and safe place to live. Sadly, the area today has a crime rate much higher than the national average, and is less than a mile from George Floyd Square, the site of Floyd's highly publicized death.

Lars and Jensine's youngest child, Valborg, was the first of their three daughters to marry. She was thirty years old when she married her fiancé Knut Andrew Holstad, a little over a year after moving to Minneapolis. Knut, like Valborg, was a first-generation American born to Norwegian immigrants. The two were wed on October 15, 1913, at Bethlehem Lutheran Church. Revered Green had the proud honor of officiating his youngest daughter's wedding on that crisp autumn day during the peak foliage of the Minnesota leaves.

The Green Home. 3152 Elliot Ave. Minneapolis.
Photo Credit: www.google.com/maps. 2025.

On July 11, 1917, Reverend Green replied to a letter from Elling and Anna Haug's daughter. Reverend Green had married the Haugs thirty-five years prior, and their daughter wrote to invite him to their thirty-fifth anniversary party. The letter was translated from Norwegian and is on record in both original and translated form at the Watonwan County Historical Society.

Minneapolis Minn. July 11, 1917

Dear Miss Haug,

Received your letter, thanks!

Just think, your parents have lived together 35 years. That is a long time. Also raised and trained so many children; all conducted themselves well. This is much to thank God for, as children are a present from God. Yes, "Mamma" and I have lived together 48 years the 8th of Nov. Time passes on never to return. God give that when our journey ends we may have used our days well. I had baptized all of you, confirmed most of you, and accompanied one or two to the grave. Your father and I were friends for 40 years, we shared pioneer life and were in God's standing with each other. My home community is not easily forgotten, my home for many years. I will arrive in Madelia 9 P.M. no doubt. You will be crowded so I could stay overnight at J. Lee or A.B. Anderson. I leave home Sat. forenoon, stop at St. Peter for sick calls at the hospital then to Madelia on the 9 o'clock train.

Greetings to "Pa and Ma" and family and thanks for the invitation.

Respectfully

L. E. Green

A week after the signage of the armistice agreement which brought an end to the First World War, Reverend Green walked another daughter down the aisle. He and Jensine's second oldest daughter, Marie, married her husband Peter Percival Perrin on November 20, 1918. They were both forty years old when they exchanged vows in the family home at 3152 Elliot Avenue, as recorded in the church records. The wedding was officiated not by her father, but by Reverend C. K. Solberg of Bethlehem Lutheran, the family's church.

Marie's new husband Peter was a British man, born in London, and an immigrant to the United States. He was also a Presbyterian minister, a fact that likely caused many long, heartfelt discussions between family members. Marie's sister Valborg and her husband Knut signed as witnesses.

The 1920 U.S. Census shows Lars, Jensine, and their oldest daughter Annie living at the family home on Elliot Avenue. Annie was the couple's only child who never married. Also in the home at the time was a sixty-five-year-old boarder named Edward Eckman. He was a bank bookkeeper and a widower who had emigrated from Sweden in his mid-forties.

The 1920 census gives the year Reverend Green became a naturalized American citizen: 1902. At nearly eighty years old, Lars and his loving Jennie appeared to be living a healthy, happy retirement. In the days before Social Security, and with daughter Annie unemployed, the income from Mr. Eckman's lodging was a blessing to the family.

The following letter was written by Revered Green in 1923, during his retirement in Minneapolis. At the time of its writing, it had been exactly fifty years since he first arrived to the Hanska–Madelia area. So much had changed in the course of that time. In it, he recounts several memories and stories of life for the early pioneers. It can be found in the research library at the Brown County Historical Society and Museum in New Ulm, Minnesota.

REV. LARS E. GREEN'S LETTER on EARLY DAYS

(Written to Petra Lien Molmen in 1923 after his retirement. Lonesome in retirement, she suggested he write to her about earlier days. In 1959 the Norwegian letter was in the possession of Emil Hage in New Ulm, who is now deceased. Mrs. Molmen died in 1961.)

I think the letter has great historical value. For one thing it helps us appreciate what ditching, tiling, and road building has done for our community. Lees for instance no longer live on an island.

The Revered Green was pastor of Lake Hanska and surrounding congregations from 1873–1900. He again served while we were without a pastor in 1910–1911. Thus he has performed the service of baptism, confirmation, marriage for my mother and baptism and confirmation for me.
My appreciation to the Backens for making our community a community. -- Petra

(Translation from Norwegian by Petra Lien Molmen)

Dear Petra Lien:

Thanks for your dear letter and the suggestion that I write a little about the olden days in and around Madelia and Lake Hanska. I shall attempt to write a few memoirs.

I shall then in the first place give the reason why I became a minister. When I was twenty years old I was converted. It was the word of God: "Awake, you who sleep, arise from the dead, and Christ shall enlighten your path." — Ep. 5:14. When I, by the grace of God, could experience how good it was to have learned to know Jesus as a Savior, and how necessary it was for everybody to turn to God, I began to talk to others about this, talked especially to my former pals, who were servants of sin.

A desire came to me to read God's word, and daily pray to God. After awhile I began attending prayer meetings and tried to encourage others to conversion. In order to do this in a way that would be of greater value to others, I entered the theological school of 3–4 years and was ordained as a pastor on November 8, 1869. Then I was pastor for Wanamingo, Spring Valley congregations in Minnesota and Forest City, Iowa until the spring of 1873, when I received the call for Linden, Lake Hanska, Madelia, and Butternut Valley churches.

My trip from Forest City, one hundred miles, took three days. I used a little Indian pony whose name was "Kab" and a single buggy. This trip is easily made in three hours now by automobile. I entered the home of Jens Torson, who was then County Treasurer of Watonwan County. He gave me a ride to Frantz Lee in Lake Hanska and there I stayed about a day.

Maundy Thursday I was to preach in Albion, a short ways from Lee's, but Lee's house was on an island surrounded by a nine-mile long lake and also a big slough, so we had to drive five extra miles to get around this slough and also back again.

Well, we started out. Lee had a very good team of horses and we wanted to get over the end of the lake and there was deep water. When we got out in the middle of the lake the wagon box floated up and the water flowed over us, but the horses ran with all their might with us four men, Lee, Erick Sweine, Syver Sorgumgaard and me— four Haugianere—a good company. We arrived safely in Albion.

I went once a month, on weekdays to visit Albion, St. James, Long Lake, St. Olaf, and Rosendale. These latter congregations later became the call of A. Hagen from Norway. My trips to these congregations began on Monday to Albion, Monday evening to St. James, Tuesday to St. Olaf, Wednesday to Long Prairie, Friday to Rosendale, and so back to Madelia and Linden.

On my first trip to Rosendale I fell into the cellar. I conducted services in a little log house belonging to a Swedish man. Five or six children were to be baptized. When the fathers and mothers came inside, the house was full and the rest of the people had to stand outdoors and listen as best as they could. I had gotten into my ministerial garb and sung a hymn verse, "See Children are the Lord's

Gift." I stood there and talked to the mothers, that they should thank God that they were well again and able to come to services with their children, who through baptism were to become members of God's Kingdom. I admonished them to pray for their children, teach them God's word, and live as a good example for them. Then the floor fell down into the cellar. The cellar was full of water so the floor floated on the water and the stove stood slanting. Men outdoors heard the crashing and came to see what was the matter. Well, we stopped a while, then continued our services with the floor floating on the water. That took two or three hours. Another minister was said to have fallen in the cellar, but another way.

We had services just once a month so it couldn't be helped if it lasted a bit long. People had much more time than now to hear God's word. Afterwards we each went happily to our own.

My territory for work was at that time large, twenty miles north to south and thirty miles east to west. The territory was inhabited by Norwegians, some Germans, and Swedish Lutherans. Since I was the only minister west of St. Peter, I baptised and married Norwegians, Swedes, and Germans. The singing was always Norwegian, but it sounded like slightly varying melodies. Norwegians and Swedes were from different districts with different dialects— Telemarken, Gudbrandsdalen, Ostlandet, and Stavanger. All sang as best they could, and I do believe they sang with sincere hearts.

When in 1873 I came to Madelia, the grasshoppers came also, and they were ruinous for four years. That was hard times. People were mostly newcomers who lived in a little log house or in a cellar, and had plowed a little piece of land and sowed a little wheat, corn, potatoes, etc. The grasshoppers took everything in a day or two. People tried to get rid of them but without success until they themselves got the notion to go and then they left as fast as they came and have been gone since.

People were generally poor. Some had more than others. Many left their land and moved to other places. Money was rarely to be gotten for butter or eggs. These were sold at the store but people had to take pay in goods, or else checks for which one could trade later.

The pastor's salary was often paid with such checks. Once on Easter Sunday there was to be an offering for the minister and he got three 25-cent pieces, a total of 75 cents, but people simply had no money. When an offering amounted to 10–12 dollars, it was very much. With the minister's salary, it had to go as it could. What he couldn't get he just struck out as he figured it was his duty to share hard times. Baptisms were usually a dollar or fifty cents.

One woman told me she tried to gather so she should have a dollar for the minister when he baptized her first child. She drove twenty miles to Lake Hanska, but the minister returned the dollar and said she should buy herself some coffee. She said she never treasured a dollar so much, either before or since. At confirmation the children each gave the minister a dollar, some fifty cents. Funerals were not paid. The minister once gave each of four motherless children a dollar as he felt so sorry for them. Neither the father or the children ever forgot this. Sympathy and help when in trouble is doubly appreciated. Pay for weddings seemed much if it was three dollars. Sometimes it was a dollar or two, many times just thank you.

My first wedding in Butternut was performed in the middle of the night. It was a Danish man named Sorenson who was to marry a widow, Mrs. Stene. There was no church at that time. The ceremony was to be in the schoolhouse. Many were invited to the wedding. I came somewhat late being unfamiliar with the roads there. A big crowd stood outside and waited for me to come. I asked the bridegroom for the license. No, he didn't know that that was needed. He had come from Wisconsin and there at that time a license was not necessary, as the minister would take an oath that nothing was in the way of the marriage. I told them they had to have a license in Minnesota and to Mankato, the county seat, was twenty miles, no telephones and no automobiles. Two of the best known had to drive away in a lumber wagon. They drove eight miles to Lake Crystal and from there they telegraphed to Mankato.

The brother of the bride told me he thought there would be no wedding ceremony until the following day and that he thought it best I took my wife and children to his house to lie down and sleep and then return the following day. They evidently thought it wasn't fitting for a minister to be at a wedding all night.

There were so many people, young and old. At weddings they were often lively, and a person could never know what they might think of. They would not bring sorrow to their pastor by doing what was wrong. He had spoken against dancing and drinking at weddings. He went to this brother's house and laid down in peace. Later in the night someone pounded on our window. I asked what they wanted. Yes, now they had come with the license. And I must come and marry them before the people went home. I went and performed the marriage ceremony in the usual manner and went back.

We went to the bride's house to eat breakfast. After we had eaten I sat down to read a paper. A man came to me in working clothes. A woman asked me if that was the bridegroom. Thoughtlessly I said yes. She went and congratulated him and gave him her good wishes—the man said, "I'm not the bridegroom. I'm the hired man." The woman was ill at ease, but it was my fault. Well this was my first wedding and in the middle of the night.

There had been one wedding before in this congregation. The wedding was to be in the same schoolhouse. The minister and the bridal party was there. Some man came and whispered in the minister's ear that the bridegroom was not confirmed. The minister started to examine him to see if he had so much knowledge of his religion that he could confirm him. So confirmation was performed first, then the wedding ceremony, so it was late in the evening before the wedding dinner could be served.

Among the funerals I performed the 35–40 years I served this call, there were especially two that made such an impression on me that I never forgot them. One was a mother who died from two newborn babies. She was the sister of Jacob Bakke, married to Thore Bjornson. She lay in that black coffin with one child on each arm. They were now resting until Resurrection Morning.

The other was in Linden, funeral of K. Helling and his wife Mary. He was sickly for many years of TB. She was also sick a long time of cancer, and suffered terribly. She died first and he died a few hours afterward. They were carried to the church yard by eight of the old pioneers—to and from the Linden church near their home. Both died in the faith of their Savior and were laid side by side in the Linden Cemetery where they rest until Resurrection Morning.

I made many sick calls in those years I was pastor in and around Madelia. But one especially I remember best. Although just eight miles from home, it took me from Thursday until Sunday before I came home again. A sick man lived in a cellar near Lake Hanska. A neighbor of Iver Sten (Stone) sent a message for me. I went in the evening and served communion to him and then I was to go home. I had put my horses in at Sten's. Snow began and the wind was severe.

Mr. Sten begged me to stay overnight and the storm would subside. He knew what storms really meant in the winter, since that winter before he had lost nearly all of his cattle which had strayed and frozen to death. Well, I stayed over night. In the morning the storm and snow was such that it was almost impossible to get in the barn to give the cattle the barest necessities to keep them alive. That lasted Friday, Saturday, and until Sunday morning.

Being a little quieter I started homeward. The horses would go on the snowcrust, then they would fall through and thus we kept up for 3–4 miles before I realized it would be impossible to get home with the horses, so I put them in the barn at E. Afdem and started walking on foot home, went in to rest at N. Harmandsen a while. They wouldn't let me go any further, but I knew the folks at home were worried about me. I had a heavy fur coat and boots with handles on, such as they used at the time. Heavy it was, but it went. I went over Gove Lake and up in the woods, then the snow became so deep, I couldn't walk, but had to pull myself forward, and my boots got full of snow. Cold it was and started to get dark. Tired I was getting and weak from hunger, so I climbed up in an oak tree and sat there to rest and think—perhaps I never would come home to my wife and children. I prayed to God to be with both them and me.

As I sat there a while I heard a rooster crow and that made me realize I was near some home. I climbed down, went in that direction I heard the rooster and found an American home. They greeted me with great friendliness and gave me tea to drink and dry stockings for my feet. Then I only had to go by one farm and I was home.

At home, my family was greatly concerned, but a little boy who is now a minister said to Mother, "Papa will come home soon." We of course prayed for that. Now they and I were glad. My horses I couldn't get home for about ten days because of snow drifts in the roads.

That was a different winter for many people. We couldn't get to the church yard with the dead for two or three weeks. On one occasion, they had to pull the corpse to the churchyard (cemetery) on a sled. Another instance, they dug the coffin into the snow until it should be possible to get to the churchyard. The man in this instance died in the night when I visited him.

There were not fine parsonages waiting for a minister to come and see if it was good enough. Stub, Koren, and others had to be thankful to live for a long time with some family. At that time there was no parsonage in this call. The Reverend Tore Hattrem who was pastor there before me lived with farmers until he died in the big storm which crossed Minnesota and other states the seventh, eighth, and ninth of January, 1873. Many people and animals froze to death.

Now the minister should have a house and they managed to rent a house for him which had been used the previous winter for storing wheat. The plastering was broken and rat holes here and there—in fact the place had been a feast house for rats. Now they were going to tear down what was left of the plastering and start over. We of course had to live in this house while it was being done, even if it was both dusty and damp. The house of course was cold, having no storm windows or double doors, and no foundation, the house was set on a few stones. So came the winter with snow and cold weather. A straw stable was also part of the house, but it was also cold.

*We had a horse, a cow, and a few chickens. I got a boy to stay
with us in the winter to take care of this, chop wood, etc. I asked him
once how the chickens were getting along. He said "They are all dead
except one." I shook my head and said no more about it.*

*Late in the winter the boy came in the house and said: "A
newcomer has come to us during the night." My wife said: "Where
does he come from?" Answer: "He comes from the barn. He is a nice
beautiful calf, but in the barn he will freeze to death, we have to take
him in the kitchen." "Oh, but that cannot be possible," she said. "Oh
yes," the boy said, "that is often done here." "Well," she said, "we
better do that then, but how will we get him in?" "Oh, I carry him
in." So he found a sack, tied it around the calf, carried him and laid
him on the floor. The children looked at the animal and thought he
was a pretty creature. The calf lay still awhile then pulled himself
under the table which stood with cups and other dishes since
breakfast. After awhile the calf raised up under the table and the table
fell over with everything on it.*

*My wife, out in the dining room, heard the crash, looked out
into the kitchen, and there lay the table overturned, with the cups and
other dishes on the floor. Milk and water flowed onto the floor. The
children ran to each their corner like so many scared birds. The calf
got up and looked at them as if nothing was wrong, and as if he would
say: I can't help this. You took me in without my asking.
My wife hollered to the boy that he had to take the calf out again
whether he lived or died. The boy took him out. He became nice and
big, but was soon consumed by meat eaters. Well, this was the first
Norwegian parsonage in the territory.*

*When we look back 50–60 years and compare the present
times, and think of the changes that have come about in all ways, we
wonder how it has all happened. If one left Lake Hanska or Linden in
1873 and came back in 1923, he would wonder if it was the same
place. Where I was the only pastor, there are now five pastors and all
have plenty to do. There are built thirteen Norwegian churches where
there was one half-built one, and no parsonage. Now there are five
parsonages.*

In 1873, everybody was poor, now nearly everybody is well-off, some even rich, owners of 25 to 100 thousand dollars. A man died a few years ago for whom I had performed a marriage ceremony in another's home. For another one I baptized his first child in a dugout, but at this death he owned about 60 thousand dollars. Others own even more. So we must say, "The Lord has been good and let our work succeed with His blessing," so in America it is good to be—as far as material things are concerned. As far as the spiritual goes, the Lord knows his own in both Norway and America, yes in the whole world.

My first friends from 1873 are now mostly dead: Eric Sveine, L. Sorumgaard, Peder Brandli, P. Thormodson, Ole Stone, the Thordson Brothers are gone. A few are still living, F. Lee, Lars Synes, Ole Bjorgen, etc.

It might be interesting for you to know a little about your grandparents. P. Brandli came to America from Lesjoskogen, Gulbrandsalem, with his wife and child (Mrs. Ole Sletta). They lived at first in a little house in the Bezeer grove, three or four miles north of Madelia. In this house there were eighteen newcomers. It is told that some of them had to stand while others could lie down to rest.

Mrs. Brandli died leaving her husband and a little daughter. Mrs. Brandli was buried at the Linden cemetery. After a few years Brandli wrote to a Christian girl in Norway, asking her if she could come and be his wife. She came and that was the last one that Reverend Hattrem married. Both of your grandparents were very sincere Christians, but they had very different natures. His was quiet, said little, and was a genuine Israelite in who there was no guile. Therefore, it was commonly said: "If there was a true Christian it is Peter Brandli."

He was often our leader in singing and led us often at prayer meetings. He died in faith in Jesus many years ago. Mrs. Brandli was more of a talker and admonished others to conversion, she was thorough in her Christianity if somewhat frank in speaking her opinion. She died in faith in Jesus this year. Over her coffin, one minister spoke over the words: "She did what she could." Another—

"Blessed are the dead who die in the Lord." I am hoping some day to meet your grandparents in Heaven.

At the first church services my wife attended, her eye met a tall grave monument with this inscription: O Father, how we long to see each other again. This was the first monument ever raised over a Norwegian pastor in America, now there are many over pastors' graves. The Reverend Hattrem died in January 1872*. In the spring of 1873 this statue was erected in loving memory of him: it was a good thing they acted while the iron was hot and had it completed before the grasshoppers came. [*The correct year of Reverend Hattrem's death is 1873.]

Before services, my wife with the two little girls went over to a house and asked if she could get a little water. The woman answered, there was water by the pole – or pump. Then she asked if these children were from far away, they were so sun-tanned. Who in the world were these children? My wife answered that they are the minister's children. But he has such small children, he that looks so old, but perhaps he has a young wife. Oh, I am his wife, answered my wife. Oh are you that, well, would you like some coffee? Then she said to my little girl, Are you the daughter of the minister, well surely you shall get cream too, you. Then she ran down the cellar to get cream. This Maria got to hear often in her lifetime: Are you the daughter of the preacher, believe me you shall get cream too, you.

It was quite common to drink beer and whiskey in those times and I had to talk against it and work to get the saloons out of the towns. Not everybody liked this and some blasphemed. A couple of times I had to go into a saloon and get hold of a man whose wife and children stood outside and wept. The man came out and said: You found me in a bad place now. He went with them.

Some years later I was driving home and I met a wagon with two boys in. My horse was in the habit of stopping whoever he met and did also at this time. One of the boys took up a bottle and said haughtily: "Would you like a drink?" "Yes," I said. He gave me the bottle and he said, "Now don't drink it all up." I took the bottle and knocked it against the buggy wheel so glass and whiskey flew in all directions. Then I hit the horse with the buggy whip and drove away. They drove away and perhaps didn't say any nice words. One of them got diphtheria and died a few weeks afterwards. The other came after awhile, wept and asked forgiveness. Hope he became after that a new person and sought God until his death.

If I should tell everything it would be too long to read and remember.
L. E. Green

Reverend Green not only performed the joyous ceremonies of marriage and baptism for his community and his own family, but he somberly and dutifully performed their funerals and burials as well. Sadly, he was called upon as not only uncle, but as pastor, to help oversee the funerals of his two nephews, Bernhard and Olaf. The two little boys he met so many years ago when they first arrived from Norway, he also helped lay to rest when illness took them both during middle age.

Bernhard, whose wedding Reverend Green officiated at Linden Lutheran, was laid to rest at that same church when he died on June 28, 1916, from tuberculosis. Bernhard's daughters, Cora and Ada, would be buried beside their father years later.

Reverend Green's nephew Olaf, who married at Trinity Lutheran in 1900, was laid to rest at that same church when he died from encephalitis on May 8, 1928. The two brothers, who had been wed weeks apart by their uncle, both passed away less than a year from each other as well. Olaf lived on Summit Avenue in Hanska village, and was a member of the church choir. He had also worked as a clerk at The Farmer's Store in town.

The third nephew, Frithjof, who was wed by Reverend Green in 1900, also passed away while the reverend was living in Minneapolis after retirement. Frithjof died from tuberculosis in 1929 at his farmhouse in Linden, and is buried at the Nora Unitarian Universalist Cemetery.

Four years after Reverend Green first wrote to Petra Lien with his memoir letter, he wrote again on March 29, 1927. He told her that at eighty-six years of age he had "wishes for Jesus to come soon." He remembered his first service in the Torkjell Helling cabin—fifty-four years prior. He fondly remembered the Sorumgaards, Ingebrigt and Jakob Bakke, Per and Brit Brandli, Erik Sveine, the Synstebys, and the Fredricksons.

The roaring twenties were quiet and peaceful for the Green Family, as not many records of their activities and lives exist. One exception, however, is the widely celebrated coverage of Lars and Jensine's sixtieth wedding anniversary.

The Watonwan County Historical Society has a clipping from *The Minneapolis Star* newspaper that ran an article of the special day in 1929. Not only was it the couple's wedding anniversary, the date was also the sixtieth anniversary of the reverend's ordainment as a Lutheran pastor as well.

Couple Marks Double 60th Anniversary

Still eager to discuss current events after watching the northwest pass from pioneer days to the modern period, the Rev. and Mrs. Lars E. Green, 3152 Elliot Avenue, will celebrate Friday what they term the 'greatest day of their lives"—their sixtieth wedding anniversary and the sixtieth anniversary of Mr. Green's ordination as a minister.

The fact that they are both 89 years old, did not deter the couple in preparing for the joint celebration. Mrs. Green is so enthusiastic about the event that she is planning to wear the wedding slippers she wore when they were married in 1869 in Chicago. They will hold open house at their home Friday and friends from throughout the city as well as other sections of the state are expected to visit them. Their three daughters and only son will bring their eight grandchildren to the party, too.

Mr. Green was pastor of four churches combined in Forest City and Wanamingo, Minnesota for several years, but was called later to the pastorate of the Norwegian Lutheran church at Madelia. His last pastorate was at Lake Hanska, Minn, from which he retired in 1912, coming to the city. His son, the Rev. J. M. Green of Chicago is president of the eastern district of the Norwegian Lutheran churches of America. — The Minneapolis Star, November 5, 1929

Reverend Lars and Jensine Green, both 89 years old, celebrating their 60th wedding anniversary at their home in Minneapolis, MN. Jensine is wearing her wedding slippers from 1869. Photo Credit: The Minneapolis Star, Nov. 5, 1929.

The 1930 US Census was taken five months after the couple's double celebration, and one week before Reverend Green's eighty-ninth birthday. Lars and Jensine's advanced age had begun to catch up with them. Their daughter Valborg and her husband Knut had moved

103

into the family home to help Annie care for their elderly parents. Knut was working as a treasurer for a publishing house, while Valborg and Annie cared for the day-to-day activities of the home and its occupants.

Reverend Green turned eighty-nine years old on Easter Sunday, April 20, 1930. *The Minneapolis Star* ran the following article on April 18 in honor of the event:

Easter Sunday Is the 89th Birthday of Lutheran Pastor Rev. L. E. Green

Reverend L.E. Green, 3152 Elliott Avenue, will celebrate his eighty-ninth birthday on Easter Sunday. Rev. Green is the second oldest pastor of the Norwegian Lutheran church. Rev. Green was born April 20, 1841, and was ordained into the ministry in 1869. He has served parishes at Forest City, Iowa; Lake Hanska, Minn., and Madelia, Minn. He was married to Miss Jensine Jenson in 1869. They celebrated their sixtieth wedding anniversary last fall. Rev. Green served as circuit president for 10 years and as circuit supervisor for three years. Rev. and Mrs. Green have made their home in Minneapolis since 1912. He is the father of Rev. Joseph Green of Chicago, district president of the eastern district of the Church of America, of Mrs. K. A. Holstad, whose husband is assistant treasurer at the N. L. (Norwegian Lutheran) Church of America, and of Miss Anna Green who lives with her parents. —The Minneapolis Star, April 18, 1930.

Over the course of his lifetime, Reverend Green's April birthday was shared with Easter Sunday on a handful of occasions. Sadly, 1930 would be the fifth and final Easter birthday he would have.

Lars Engebretsen Green passed away at home on Monday, June 9, 1930, at 3:45 p.m. The amazing life of one of God's finest servants had come to an end. The reverend had been suffering from colon cancer for at least three years, according to his death certificate.

His passing came six weeks after his birthday celebration. A brief funeral service was held in his home on June 11, 1930, at 3 p.m. Immediately afterwards, his remains were brought to Madelia, where a large service, widely attended by the community, took place on Thursday, June 12, at 1 p.m.

The Watonwan County Historical Society has a clipping of his obituary. It doesn't show the paper that published the article, but it was likely *The Madelia Times Messenger.*

Rev. L. E. Green Is Called to Last Rest

Although he was more than 89 years old, still the news of the death of Rev L.E. Green, former much beloved pastor and highly respected citizen of this community, came as a shock to the many old friends of the veteran minister. Following a brief illness Rev. Mr. Green passed peacefully away at his home in Minneapolis, Monday afternoon June 9th, 1930. He was the second oldest pastor in the Norwegian Lutheran church of America.

Lars Engebretsen Green was born at Romerike, Norway, April 20, 1841, and in 1866 immigrated to America. He attended Augustana Seminary at Paxton, Illinois, from 1866 to 1869, and Concordia Seminary at St. Louis in 1873. His first charge as pastor was at Forest City, Iowa, where he labored in the Lord's vineyard from 1869 to 1873. In 1873 he was called to Madelia. He accepted the call and lived for a number of years in Linden township. The parish consisted of the congregations of Hanska, Butternut, Linden and Madelia, and he served many more congregations temporarily. At one time he served a stretch of country extending from St. Peter to Odin. In 1912 Rev. Mr. Green resigned his position here, retired from the ministry, and moved to Minneapolis, where he has since made his home. After a long life of untiring devotion in the service of his Creator, a good and faithful servant has been called to his eternal rest. Mr. Green is survived by his faithful wife, whom he married in 1869, and by four children, Annie Green and Mrs. K.A. Holstad of Minneapolis; Mrs. P. P. Perrin of Solland, Minnesota, and Joseph M. Green of Chicago, president of the Eastern district of the Norwegian Lutheran church of America.

The remains were brought to Madelia for burial, and funeral services were held at Trinity Lutheran church at 1 o'clock Thursday afternoon. The church was crowded to capacity and many were unable to gain admittance. The memory of this good pastor will long be cherished in the hearts of his former parishioners and other friends and the sincere sympathy of this community goes out to the sorrowing wife and children.

In 1954, Lake Hanska Lutheran Church member Petra Lien Molmen lovingly created an album of snipped articles that became periodicals for *The New Ulm Journal*. On June 24, 1954, she wrote the article titled *Lake Hanska Church History*, "*...then began the long career of Pastor L. E. Green who served from 1873–1900 then again from 1910–1911. Part of pioneer landscape is Reverend Green and his little pony "Kab." Doctor Cooley of Madelia once made the remark that he took care of people's bodies and Reverend Green of their souls.*"

Reverend Green cared deeply about his community, and they reciprocated his devotion. He lived beside them in poverty, foregoing a salary many times, when he could have lived a comfortable upper-class life in Norway. Lars Green dedicated his life to the service of God and to others. He lived a life of bravery, sacrifice, humility, and generosity. When his life ended, after nearly ninety years on Earth, he was finally at rest. His words and actions touched and inspired thousands of lives, and those virtues have lived on throughout the generations.

Reverend Green's dearest Jensine, who had crossed the Atlantic with him in 1866, and endured so many hardships and so much loss during their years on the prairie, continued to live at the Minneapolis home she and Lars shared for another two years before she passed. Her death came on March 14, 1932, at 3:00 a.m. She had suffered a stroke in January, and slowly lingered for the next two months. She and Lars' son, Reverend Joseph Green, traveled from his Wisconsin home to see his ailing mother a week before her passing. Joseph knew that would be the last time he would see her alive.

As Jensine slipped into a coma and became unresponsive, her faithful son said his final goodbye. While at his mother's deathbed he received word that he urgently needed to return home. Joseph's oldest son, twenty-five-year-old Rolf, had been bedridden from an unknown illness for the past five months. He had suddenly taken a turn for the worst.

Sadly, Joseph would lose both his mother and his firstborn child within the same day. A funeral was held for Jensine at her Minneapolis home, followed by a second funeral the next day in Madelia. She was placed at rest beside her adoring husband at Trinity Lutheran Cemetery.

The *Madelia Times Messenger* ran an article honoring Jensine's legacy on March 18, 1932.

Mrs. L. E. Green Dies At Minneapolis Home

This community was saddened last Monday, when the news reached here that Mrs. L. E. Green, old and dearly beloved former citizen of Madelia, had passed away at her late home in Minneapolis. For 36 years Mrs. Green and her husband had lived here, and each succeeding year had brought them nearer and dearer to all with whom they came in contact.

Mrs. Green, whose maiden name was Jensine Jensen, was married to the late L. E. Green in Chicago in 1869. They came to Madelia in 1873 and made their home until 1909, when they moved to Minneapolis. Mrs. Green died Sunday night, March 13th, from the infirmities of age. She is survived by four children; Anna of Minneapolis; Joseph, of Mt. Horeb, Wisconsin, president of the Eastern district of the Norwegian Lutheran Church of America; Marie (Mrs. P. Percival Perrin) of South Dakota and Valborg (Mrs. K. A. Holstad) of Minneapolis. Five grandchildren also survive her.

Funeral services were conducted at Trinity Lutheran church in Madelia, at 1:30 Thursday afternoon, March 17th. Rev. Reigstad of Bethlehem Lutheran Church, Minneapolis, officiated, assisted by Rev. Mr. Syrdal of Madelia. The remains were laid to rest in the Lutheran cemetery, beside those of her husband.

MRS. JENSINE GREEN RITES WEDNESDAY

Funeral services for Mrs. Jensine Green, 90 years old, 3152 Elliot Avenue, will be held at the home at 3 p.m., Wednesday, and at 1 p.m., Thursday, at Madelia. Mrs. Green was the widow of the late Rev. L. E. Green, pioneer pastor of the Norwegian Lutheran Church of America.

She was born in Oslo, Norway and came to America in 1866. She lived at Madelia for 38 years and in Minneapolis for the past 20 years. Survivors are one son, Rev. J. M. Green, bishop of the eastern district of the Norwegian Lutheran Church, and three daughters, Mrs. P. P. Perrin of Yankton, S.D.; Anna Green and Mrs. K. A. Holstad of Minneapolis.— The Minneapolis Star, Tuesday, March 15, 1932.

After Reverend Green and Jensine had both passed, the community they had faithfully served for so many decades came together to honor the couple's legacy. In the fall of 1932, six months after Jensine's passing, hundreds of congregation members from Lake Hanska, Linden, Butternut, and Trinity Lutheran Churches gathered to immortalize the loving pair.

The pews and auditorium were filled to capacity. Hundreds of chairs were brought in for the overflow of people. The flock first gathered at Lake Hanska Lutheran, where Reverend Joseph Green delivered the blessed sermon. From there, everyone caravanned to Trinity Lutheran Cemetery for the unveiling of the monument dedicated to Reverend Green's long years of service.

GREEN MEMOMRIAL SERVICES HELD

Sunday Morning September 25, 1932, Norwegian Lutherans from the Hanska vicinity gathered at the Lake Hanska church to honor the memory of the sainted couple, Rev. and Mrs. L. E. Green, pioneer church workers in these parts. Long before the appointed hour for services every available pew in gallery and church auditorium was filled. Several hundred chairs were drafted into service to care for the vast congregation that had assembled.

108

The festival sermon was delivered by the Right Reverend Joseph Green, son of Rev. and Mrs. L. E. Green and President of the Eastern District of the Norwegian Lutheran Church. In his inspiring and encouraging message Bishop Green dwelt on the manifold spiritual blessing which had come to us through the faithful endeavors of the pioneer laymen and pastors. He reminded the congregation of the riches which had come to us through the Kingdom of God. These treasures were to be preferred to the transitory material treasures offered by the world. The Bishop stated further: "The trials through which we are passing will under God only make us more kind, sympathetic and tender in our dealings with our fellow creatures."

The preacher spoke feelingly about the untiring efforts of his sainted father in breaking the Bread of Life to his people in these parts in the early days. The President's sermon was very well received. Rev. G. Oppen, Lake Crystal, conducted the alter services. The joint chorus under the relationship, relatives and friends of the family from the Twin Cities and other points, the visiting clergy and their families and the committees on monument from the four congregations by a group of ladies from the Western and Southern Aids. The hostesses of the day had all received Confirmation at the hands of the pioneer pastor.

At 3 P.M. a still larger congregation had assembled at the Madelia Lutheran cemetery for the impressive unveiling ceremonies. Rev. G. Oppen led in scripture reading and prayer and consecrated the recently acquired portion of the Madelia cemetery as a Christian burying ground. The chorus rendered an appropriate anthem. Two little boys, James and Joseph Green, Mt. Horeb, Wis., sons of the Bishop and grandsons of the late Rev. L. E. Green, unveiled the monument. Rev. P. R. Syrdal, Madelia, spoke about the labors of Rev. L. E. Green and dedicated the monument to his memory. Rev. V. F. Larson, Hanska, read the inscriptions on the Memorial, pointed out the noteworthy features of this particular stone and explained the various emblems and symbols that had been engraved upon the face of the stone. Rt. Rev. Joseph Green delivered the closing address. The Congregation sang: "O taenk naar engang samles skal." Rev Syrdal pronounced the apostolic benediction.

    Beautiful fall flowers and memorial wreaths graced the Lake Hanska church and the family lot of Madelia. The memorial, which is a work of art, comes from the hand of Harold Bjork, Minneapolis, designer of monuments. The pattern is new and pleasing to the eye. The lines are simple and graceful. A tall, stately, granite shaft rises from a well-proportioned base and points to the heavens above, the abode of God. The memorial is made of Barre granite from the quarries of Vermont. It stands nine feet and four inches high and weights three and a half tons. It bears the following inscription: "In memory of faithful and unselfish service. 1873 and 1911. John 3:16. Landstads salme 94. The Blood of Jesus Christ, His Son, Cleaneth us from all Sin. " Appropriate foot stones with names and dates mark the two graves.— The Hanska Herald September 30, 1932.

Reverend Lars Green Gravesite Monument, Trinity Lutheran Cemetery, Madelia, MN. Photo Credit: Author's Personal Collection

*T*he cold winter had long ended and spring was in full bloom when Reverend Green was laid to rest. The mourning guests had departed, and all was quiet and peaceful among the acres of the dearly departed. The days stretched longer, warmer, and brighter with the coming of summer. And all was still. As it was then, just as it is today.

Scattered wildflowers of yellow, pink, and purple continue to bloom amidst the tall grasses of the prairie headstones. Humming bumblebees land gently upon the soft petals. In the distance, the summer songs of the meadowlarks and sparrows break the silence. They pause briefly, then resume their quiet symphonies. Life continues all around the countryside.

It has been nearly a hundred years since Reverend Green died on that early June afternoon. In his lifetime, he experienced ample abundance as well as unbelievable loss. He knew both joyful blessings and deep heartache. He knew two different worlds—not only two separate countries and cultures, but he witnessed the progression from wagons to trains to automobiles to airplanes. He saw electricity, plumbing, and radio become commonplace in every home. He lived during an era of American history that can never be repeated. He was a pioneer, as were so many of our family's ancestors who left the only home they'd ever known for a strange and dangerous new land.

Reverend Lars Green lived a selfless life of devotion to his community and to God. He gave all he had to help others. There was not a Norwegian Lutheran church within Brown, Watonwan, or Blue Earth Counties and beyond that was unknown to him or that he didn't help establish. He is eternally resting among the other pioneers he knew and loved: his family, his friends, and his beloved congregations. His legacy lives on in the kindly people of Hanska and Madelia—whose families have been tied to the land for generations.

When you drive down the back roads of Brown and Watonwan Counties, and see his old country churches standing proudly on the open prairie, just as they had when he lived—you will find him. And he will be smiling down from Heaven.

111

"When we look back fifty to sixty years and compare the present times, and think of the changes that have come about in all ways, we wonder how it has all happened.....as far as the spiritual goes, the Lord knows his own in both Norway and America...When I, by the grace of God, could experience how good it was..."

— Reverend Lars E Green, 1923

Reverend Lars E. Green 1841–1930

His Four Children

*B*etween the birth of Reverend Green and Jensine's first child Anna Emelia in 1870 and their last child Nellie Elise in 1884, the couple lost four young daughters, all under the age of six, during the family's pioneering years. Today, the very idea of losing a single child is horrific, let alone four. In the nineteenth century, it was rare to find any family unaffected by such tragedy. Four of Lars and Jensine's children survived into adulthood—their children, their children's children, and their great-grandchildren carry on the legacy of the pioneer pastor from Norway.

Annie

The Greens' first daughter, Anna Emelia, was born in Wanamingo, Minnesota, on August 22, 1870, during the reverend's first call following seminary. As a toddler she moved with her family to Madelia, where she spent her childhood and early adulthood. In 1912, at the age of forty-two, she moved with her parents to Minneapolis. "Annie," as she was called by loved ones, never had a career, never married, nor had any children. She cared for her parents in their old age, living with them until both had passed. To pay the bills following their deaths, Annie rented out the unused rooms of her house to boarders, usually single female teachers. She remained in the family home until November 23, 1952, when she fell down the stairs and sustained a head injury. She died at eighty-two years of age, and is buried in Trinity Lutheran Cemetery.

Joseph

Joseph Marinus Green, the only son of the eight children born to the reverend and his wife, arrived on February 17, 1877. Madelia was the only home Joseph knew before he left the family farm to follow in his father's footsteps and become a Lutheran pastor. He attended college first at St. Olaf in Northfield, Minnesota, followed by the Luther Theological Seminary in St. Paul.

Joseph was married on June 15, 1905 in Winneshiek, Iowa, to Agnes Estrem at the Washington Prairie Lutheran Church. They had three sons: Rolf (born 1906), Amos (born 1907), and Orval (born 1909). The family lived in Dane County, Wisconsin, in the towns of Perry and Mount Horeb. Tragically, Agnes died on Joseph's thirty-sixth birthday, leaving him alone to raise three young sons. He married for the second time on August 26, 1919, to a widow who was also named Agnes—Agnes Dahl Pitts. Joseph had two more sons with his second wife—James was born in 1921, followed by Joseph in 1925. In 1929, Joseph became president of the Eastern District of the Norwegian Lutheran Church of America, having served as vice president for two years.

Sadly, two of Joseph's sons died as young adults. The first to pass was Rolf, who died the same day as his grandmother Jensine, following a prolonged unknown illness. Only six months later, Joseph's son Orval died due to complications from an appendectomy.

Four years after leading the service honoring the lives of both his parents, Joseph lost his own life at the age of fifty-nine on June 25, 1936. After suffering a massive stroke at home in Mount Horeb, Wisconsin, he was brought to the hospital in Madison, where he passed shortly afterward. He is buried in Daleyville, Wisconsin in the Perry Lutheran Cemetery.

Reverend Joseph M. Green. 1877–1936.
Photo Credit: Rev. Joseph Green's Grandson, Joseph Green.

Marie

Fifteen months after Joseph was born, daughter Marie Josephine Green was welcomed into the family on May 15, 1878, in Madelia. When she was thirty-four years old, her parents and two adult sisters moved to Minneapolis, but she stayed behind in Hanska. Marie was a registered nurse and midwife who delivered several babies of Brown, Watonwan, and Blue Earth Counties into the world, including the three children of the pastor who replaced her father at Lake Hanska Lutheran. She was highly educated for a woman of her time. According to her obituary, she was a graduate of Augustana College of the Evangelical Lutheran Church. She received her nurse training at Swedish Hospital in Minneapolis. Marie left the prairie in 1918, and moved into the family's Elliot Avenue home in Minneapolis.

Marie may have assumed that, like her sister Annie, she would never marry, but at the age of forty she fell in love and married a British man named Peter Percival Perrin on November 20, 1918. The couple was wed in the family home. Marie's new husband was also a minister, but unlike her Lutheran father, Peter was a Presbyterian. The newlyweds moved to Yankton, South Dakota soon after the wedding. Their son Donald Franklin was born in 1920, followed by a daughter, Neva Ruth, eight years later in Kansas. Amazingly, Marie was almost fifty years old when her daughter was born. Despite her husband's ministry, Marie baptized and raised her two children in the Lutheran faith.

The 1940 U.S. Census shows Marie and her family in Browns Valley, Minnesota, where she was working as a nurse and Peter as a minister. Two years later, in 1942, she became a widow. She and her daughter Ruth then moved to Kansas City, Missouri, to be closer to her son Donald. She remained there for the rest of her life, traveling often to Minnesota to visit family and friends. Marie died on February 15, 1957, at seventy-eight years old. Her cause of death was pneumonia related to gallbladder cancer. She and Peter are both buried at Trinity Lutheran Cemetery in Madelia.

Valborg

The youngest child of Reverend Green and Jensine was Valborg Wilhelmine Green, born on January 15, 1882 in Madelia, where she grew up with her siblings on the farm. She moved with her parents and sister Annie to the Elliot Avenue home in 1912, when she was thirty years old. Soon after, she met Knut Andrew Holstad, and the pair were married the following year on October 15, 1913, at Bethlehem Lutheran Church. The couple, known as "Andrew" and "Valla," never had children. They moved back into the Elliot Avenue home in the mid-1920s to help Annie care for their elderly parents, and they continued to live in the house for the duration of their marriage.

Andrew became the assistant treasurer of the Norwegian Lutheran Church in 1925, a position he held until his death shortly before Christmas in 1940. Valla had an extensive career in the church. According to her obituary in *The Minneapolis Star*, "she was an active church worker. She had been president of the Lutheran Women's Welfare League, southern Minnesota district, and international president of the Women's Missionary Federation, ELCA. She had served as president of the Fairview Hospital auxiliary."

After her husband's passing, Valla moved to Tacoma, Washington, where she was the assistant dean of women at Pacific Lutheran University from 1944 until her retirement ten years later. While she served at PLU, she was known as "House Mother," as stated in the university yearbook.

After her tenure, she moved back to Minneapolis, where she lived another three years until her passing on November 5, 1957. At seventy-five years old, Valborg was in great health with no underlying conditions when she contracted the flu a week before her death. The Asian Flu of 1957 was a global pandemic that took the lives of millions of people worldwide. Although she was in good health, her lungs were unable to fight the virus and she died from pneumonia. Despite her long, prestigious career, her death certificate lists her occupation as "housewife." Her funeral was held at Bethlehem Lutheran, the family's home church since 1912.

Valla and Andrew are buried together at Trinity Lutheran in Madelia. Her death, eight months after the passing of her sister Marie, marked the conclusion of the lives of Reverend Green and Jensine's children. The lineage of Reverend Lars Green and his beloved wife Jensine live on through the descendants of the couple's four grandchildren.

Valborg W. Green Holstad. (1882–1957).
Photo Credit: Pacific Lutheran University, Date circa 1950.

118

The Journey Home

There are some things in life that cannot be easily explained. We often question if our lives are predestined by God, or if our paths are determined only by our choices and circumstances, with a healthy dose of luck mixed in. When an extraordinary event happens to us, we question if it was Spirit which had guided us toward the miraculous or simply chance and statistical coincidence. Life is wondrous in that way. It keeps us pondering, exploring, and asking the existential questions.

I wrote this biography on Reverend Lars Green after I discovered an amazing link between his life and my own. When I stumbled upon this logic-defying connection, I knew deep in my core that I had to write his story. I felt compelled to share the story of southern Minnesota's pioneering pastor from Norway—a man of deep faith who dedicated his life to serving both God and his beloved community. After two years of research, it has been my absolute honor getting to know him, and I hope that reading about his journey will inspire others as much as it has me.

L: Poulsbo, Fall 2021. Photo Credit: KShields Photography from Poulsbo.
R: Poulsbo, WA Welcome Sign. Photo Credit: Nick Hoke, 2013. Wikimedia Commons

Poulsbo, Washington is an enchanting harbor town nestled along Liberty Bay on the beautiful Puget Sound. It was founded by Norwegian settlers in the 1880s and is known as Washington's "Little Norway." Its popular waterfront and small independent shops along Front Street are treasured by locals. But the secret of this charming gem has escaped, and in recent years Poulsbo has become a magnet for tourists, who come to experience its bucolic charm and old-style Scandinavian architecture.

The line of people outside Sluys Bakery is often out the door and down the sidewalk. People flock to purchase their fresh lefse, amazing donuts, and regionally famous Poulsbo Bread. The boardwalk along the bay is perfect for strolling to take in the saltwater air, or sitting on the benches to enjoy the harbor sights while the seagulls call. The waterfront gazebo hosts musical and cultural events throughout the year, including traveling groups from Norway.

King Olaf V of Norway visited Poulsbo in the fall of 1975 to celebrate Norwegian immigration to America. Another famous visitor was drawn to Poulsbo in the summer of 1994. John F. Kennedy Jr. and his fiancé Carolyn Bessette arrived by private boat to enjoy a sunset meal at That's-A-Some Italian restaurant along the waterfront. Until the restaurant's closing in 2021, people would often request to sit at "Table 1" in order to dine in the exact spot the notable couple had. The wall next to Table 1 was immortalized with a black and white photo that commemorated the day.

Every May during Syttende Mai, Poulsbo hosts its annual Viking Fest and Parade which draws boaters and spectators from all around the Puget Sound and beyond. The first Saturday of December each year, the Sons of Norway, whose lodge was built along the waterfront, host Julefest—the traditional festival that welcomes the winter solstice. At sunset, the Santa Lucia Bride, adorned in her long white gown and crown of candles, arrives in a wooden longboat, escorted by the torchlight of the Sons in their full Viking dress, who then light the bonfire before captivated spectators. Poulsbo is a magical town to visit and an incredible place to live.

My husband Noah and I met in high school and had both grown up in the neighboring city of Bremerton. We moved to Poulsbo in 1998, when our oldest son was three years old and our youngest son just a newborn. It was a fantastic place to raise young children, and we loved our years there, but Noah and I were ready to experience other parts of the country as well. Seeking both change and adventure, we sold our little Poulsbo house in the spring of 2006.

We were looking to move to a Midwestern state that had cheaper houses, good healthcare, good schools, and a low crime rate. We chose Minnesota. We liked that Noah's family had a vacation cottage in Red Wing, on the Mississippi River. Noah carried deeply fond memories of summers at the cottage as a kid. I'd heard so much about it that I was excited to finally get the chance to experience it. By moving to Minnesota, I hoped our kids would create some of the same wonderful memories: boating and swimming in Lake Pepin, sitting on the deck at sunset watching the barges loaded with grain go by, bonfires on the beach, and being lulled to sleep by the crickets and the sound of a distant passing train.

We decided on the city of Mankato due to its size, amenities, and proximity to the Twin Cities. We packed our bags, sent the kids to their grandma's house, and flew to Minneapolis. We dedicated one weekend to looking for a new home. Unfortunately though, we didn't find anything we liked within our price range. We flew home feeling discouraged. Our realtor called later that week and informed us that there's a house for sale that we might like, except it wasn't in Mankato, it was in a little town called Hanska.

We immediately got online to research Hanska to see if it might be a good fit. We appreciated that it wasn't too long of a drive from our original destination of Mankato, and it was an even closer drive to New Ulm for schools, doctors, and shopping. One of the first things we saw was that, like our town of Poulsbo, Hanska was also known as "Little Norway." It gave us a chuckle to see that the house for sale was on Viking Avenue, the same name as the main road in Poulsbo. As we read more about Hanska, we were surprised to learn that this tiny town also had a Unitarian Universalist church in it. We were leaving behind our Unitarian Universalist church in Bremerton, so this was a welcome find. We couldn't deny the feeling that the universe was speaking to us, pulling us, beckoning us to go. We looked at photos that the realtor emailed, and we liked what we saw. It was a new double-wide manufactured on a quiet street of stick-built 1970s houses. The peaceful-looking street was lined with huge maple trees. Their tall canopies shaded the houses and were bursting with tranquility and greenery. We took the leap and bought the house, sight unseen.

In May 2006, we loaded the kids, our beloved orange cat, and our entire lives into a U-Haul and began the 1,600-mile drive across the country. We wanted to make the drive as stress-free and fun as possible, so we only drove five or six hours a day. We chose hotels with pools and free breakfasts for the kids, and stopped to see some sights along the way. We stopped at Little Big Horn in Montana, and Wall Drug and 1880 Town in South Dakota. After four memorable days on the road, our destination finally came into view. Amongst the sea of cornfields, we saw a large grove of trees slowly approaching in the distance. We were home.

Hanska, MN Sign & Stabbur. Photo Credit: Author's Personal Collection.

We knew Hanska would be small, but we were surprised at just how small it was. We felt as if we were stepping back in time. The idyllic town's main street had a small gas station, a tiny brick post office, a volunteer fire station, and a corner bar. As our U-Haul pulled into the driveway, we got to experience what a tornado siren sounded like for the very first time. The sky was blue and clear, without a cloud, raindrop, or even a breeze anywhere. We looked around confused but carried on unpacking the beds and necessities for the night. We later learned it was a scheduled drill, but what a welcome.

Exhausted and exhilarated, we settled into our new home. Country life in Hanska was very different from our West-Coast life, and we were determined to adjust. It was safe, it was quiet, and it was reminiscent of days gone by. Experiencing the four seasons in Minnesota is very unlike the west coast. The hot, humid summer had glorious thunderstorms that were fascinating albeit terrifying at times. I remember driving down Highway 13 and looking up into the brightest, cloudless blue sky I'd ever seen. It felt as if the heavens went on forever.

That summer we adopted our first dog, a rat terrier named Jack, from a veterinary office in St. Peter. He had been found lost in a cornfield, and we couldn't understand why he suddenly stopped wanting to go outside on his tether. Our house backed up to a cornfield and we assumed he was afraid of the tall corn after his last encounter, but after hanging laundry on the clothesline one day I quickly discovered the true reason. The mosquitoes in the grass were so relentless that neither human nor animal could stand them for long.

When the Fourth of July arrived, we set up chairs on the edge of town and watched the fireworks show at Hanlin Field. It was a magnificent display that we would have never been able to experience so intimately back home in Washington. Our oldest son had an insatiable appetite for books and reading, and was elated to discover he could walk from our new house to the tiny library. It was no bigger than a double-car garage, but it was full of hidden treasures.

The fall foliage was so much more beautiful than the autumn leaves back home. We could feel the changing season in the crispness of the air, and the days becoming shorter. Our youngest son joined Cub Scouts, and I got a part-time job at New Ulm High School.

When the start of school arrived, we decided to have the boys attend Lafayette Charter School. It was a forty-five-minute drive there and back every day, but it was worth it. They thrived at school. It's where they first learned the term "hot dish." They made the mistake of calling it a "casserole," and were quickly corrected. They also learned about walking tacos, Fish Fridays, and Pork Day assemblies. They couldn't understand how students had indoor recess when a few raindrops fell, but were sent outside in the snow unless it was below zero. They were accustomed to the opposite. Back home, rain was a daily norm. We could always tell non-native Washingtonians by their use of umbrellas. Rain stopped nothing in Washington, but when a few snowflakes fell from the sky the entire community came to a halt.

Although we never saw the little creature, we knew we had a field mouse living under the house that fall because we'd find his droppings in an unused bathroom drawer as well as his teeth-marks on a bar of soap.

When the first snow arrived on New Year's Eve, we weren't prepared. I remember driving home from work one afternoon as the snow picked up. It was different than the heavy, wet Washington snow we were used to, which was slushy and lasted only a few days. The road from New Ulm to Hanska is a straight twelve-mile shot. I figured the drive home from work wouldn't be that difficult because, unlike home, there weren't any icy hills to navigate, and they kept the roads plowed. About halfway home the wind and snow picked up further, and the dry flakes began to swirl upon the road. It was dizzying, nauseating and, scariest of all, disorienting. I prayed for my tires to stay on the road. I felt as long as I could feel the tires on the road amongst the sea of white and gray, I would be okay. I made it home safely.

After one snow storm, we woke to find massive drifts against the house. Noah had to climb out of a window in order to clear a path to the front door. The water in our toilet bowl froze because we forgot to leave a faucet dripping, and we ran out of propane because we didn't know that we had to check the tank. We were fish out of water. A kind neighbor took pity on Noah, who was shoveling the driveway by hand. He brought his snow blower over and had it done in less than five minutes. The neighbor said he couldn't stand watching him suffer like that anymore. We were warned that Minnesota was cold, but we were unprepared for just how absolutely frigid it was.

When we did go to church, we attended Nora Unitarian Universalist Church. Christmas at Nora was lovely. I can still see the pews full of people during the Christmas Eve service, their faces softly illuminated by the glow of a single candle held in their hands as we all sang *Silent Night* in the old country church. As visitors departed the warm church into the dark, cold night, we were all given a little gift bag. Inside was candy and trinkets for the kids, and a white wooden ornament in the shape of a snowflake with "Nora Unitarian Universalist" written on the back. I still think of that magical night every Christmas when I hang the ornament on our tree.

We found the people of Brown County to be very neighborly, but the stoic nature of their Scandinavian and German heritage was evident. We were accustomed to a more free-spirited, eclectic, and diverse lifestyle. We admired the solid, good-hearted genuineness of the people; however, we felt the cultural differences between rural Minnesotans and suburban Seattleites.

When spring arrived the following year, we knew we missed Washington. We decided to move back. Our oldest would be going into junior high that fall, and we felt we had to quickly make a decision on whether to stay or to leave. We didn't want to move the boys once they started the tumultuous, formative years of junior high. We cherished our many memories on the prairie and knew that Hanska would forever be in our hearts, but we decided to move back to Washington in the spring of 2007.

Four years later, in 2011, I began the search for my biological parents, and that's when I found the Green family. I learned that my biological mother, Monica, died in a tragic car accident in 1987, but I met her father and formed a very close relationship with him. My grandpa Rolf had lost his beloved wife, Unni, the previous year. Sadly, I would never have the chance to meet my mother or my grandmother in this life. But I would discover something truly amazing.

Rolf and Unni lived in Poulsbo at the same time we did! As we compared notes, I immediately imagined them playing tennis at the same park I would swing my boys at. I imagined all the times we likely passed each other in the grocery aisle as I pushed my two little ones in the cart. Rolf and Unni were both born in Norway, and grew up during the Nazi occupation of their country in World War II. They immigrated to North America in 1954 for their honeymoon. Their ship arrived in New York harbor under the eye of Lady Liberty. They then headed to Canada for a few years, where my mother Monica was born, before eventually setting in Seattle. I was born in downtown Seattle at Swedish Hospital, but Monica was young and unprepared to be a mother. I was given up for adoption and raised in Bremerton, an hour and a half away from Seattle. Yet somehow, Rolf, Unni and I all ended up in Poulsbo—"Little Norway"—together.

I knew I needed to visit Norway, so I made it happen in October 2015. I specifically planned to be there during what would have been my mother Monica's sixtieth birthday. I had such an amazing trip staying with cousins, touring Drammen and Oslo, visiting museums, and seeing the house and farm that my grandpa Rolf was born in and grew up in. While there, I was able to sit beside Monica's grave and tell her about myself, my family, and my life. She's buried in the most gorgeous tree-filled cemetery. As I sat there talking to her a few tears softly flowed down my cheek. I placed a small, carved metallic bird upon her headstone. The old church bells tolled, and I knew for certain that she was there with me.

Ever since childhood, I have always been fascinated by both history and genealogy. I minored in history at Washington State University, and have always been especially interested in pioneering history. As a girl I couldn't get enough of the *Little House on the Prairie* books and TV show. I'd imagine myself as little Laura on her many adventures in Walnut Grove, Minnesota. When I was eleven, I went to a week-long summer camp where we lived like pioneers: churning butter, dipping candles, cooking over an open fire and using outhouses. I loved every minute of it.

While I had extensively researched my husband Noah's family tree, I'd never looked deep into my own. Being an adoptee, genealogy brings up lots of emotions. Adoptees often feel as if they never fully belong to either family, biological or adopted. But in 2022 I decided to research my Green side. Grandpa Rolf's ninetieth birthday was coming up, and as a gift I wanted to create a booklet of his family tree for him. I was also hopeful to discover where the last name "Green" came from, because it wasn't a traditional Norwegian surname, and he didn't know its roots.

Ancestry.com had grown extensively since I first began working with the site a decade earlier, and I was delighted to see that many new records from Norway had been added since I last researched. A few days into my search I sat frozen in disbelief for what seemed like an entire minute. I couldn't stop staring at the laptop as my brain tried to process. I discovered an absolutely amazing connection that can only be described as miraculous.

My still-living Grandpa Rolf had uncles, and great-uncles, who were the early Norwegian settlers of Hanska, Minnesota. His grandfather's brother was Reverend Lars Green who helped establish the area's five Norwegian Lutheran churches, all within a few miles radius of where we lived in Hanska. Grandpa Rolf had numerous aunts and uncles who were brought over by Reverend Green from Norway who would become Hanska's earliest inhabitants.

During our time in Hanska I had inadvertently been walking in the footsteps of my family, before I even knew my roots. There are over two billion acres of land in the United States. How is it that I essentially spun the globe and landed in tiny Hanska of all places? Every day I drove upon the roads and checked my mail at the post office that was once Gustav Green's homestead. The houses built by Reverend Green's nephews were a stone's throw away. Two houses down from where we lived on Viking Ave was the family whose grandfather was raised by Karen Green, Reverend Green's sister. I could hear the church bells ring at Zion Lutheran Church as I sat in my living room, not knowing Reverend Green presided over its dedication.

On Reverend Green's way to his first call as a pastor in Wanamingo, Minnesota (before coming to Hanska), he stopped at the county seat to record his seminary credentials. This was needed in order to practice as a minister in the state of Minnesota. The name of the town that housed his credentials is Red Wing, Minnesota—the same small town where my husband Noah spent so many summers during his childhood.

When I attended Nora Unitarian, I would gaze out the windows and imagine what it felt like for the settlers who sat in those same wooden pews so many years prior. I couldn't have imagined that I had relatives buried mere feet from where I sat. I knew I had to get back to Hanska to deeper explore all this new knowledge. I planned a trip for July 2022. When I planned the trip, I knew I needed to see the five churches that Reverend Green was such an instrumental part of for so many decades. I had only planned to be in town for two days so I needed to cram as much as I could into a short amount of time. I couldn't have imagined that yet another amazing connection was waiting for me.

We booked a hotel in New Ulm. It felt odd to be driving the same roads into New Ulm that I had driven daily when we lived there, fifteen years prior. This time however, I was seeing it through a new lens. New Ulm is twelve miles outside of Hanska. It's where we'd go for gas, shopping, errands, and doctor appointments. I had an appointment at the research library of the Brown County Historical Society in New Ulm. When I arrived, I was handed an entire folder on Reverend Lars Green. I immediately devoured it. One of the papers in the folder was a letter written by Lars where he described his calling and the difficult early days as a pioneer. The folder also had newspaper articles about his life and a few photos. I made copies of everything.

After a few hours in the research library, my friend Sandy, the only friend I had made while living in Hanska, picked me up at the hotel and together the two of us made an afternoon of catching up and visiting the churches to take photos. Weeks before the trip, I had reached out to Lake Hanska Lutheran, Linden Lutheran, and Trinity Lutheran churches to see if someone could meet me so I could see inside the churches and take photos. None of them returned my messages in time. While sitting in the hotel room the previous night I tried once more. I messaged Lake Hanska Lutheran on Facebook on the slight chance I'd get a reply. Within five minutes I was told that yes, someone would meet me there at 5 p.m. the next day. I was elated. I was finally going to be inside one of the churches.

I hadn't seen Hanska in fifteen years. Sandy drove us by the house we had spent that memorable year in. It looked basically the same, but a little run-down and overgrown. The two small trees that we had in our front yard were now large trees that shaded the house significantly. Hanska is so tiny that you can drive its entirety within two minutes. After driving by and taking some pictures of the house, and making the single loop through town, we stopped at Zion Lutheran where Reverend Green performed its dedication and stone laying in 1904. It was one street over from Viking Avenue. I shook my head in amazement.

Sandy and I next headed to Lake Hanska Lutheran Church. The church was just outside of town, down a gravel road that Noah and I had never explored when we lived there. When we first moved in, I remember being invited to this church by a neighbor. The pang of not accepting that invitation stung hard in the moment.

When Sandy and I got to the church, it was a beautiful sunny day. It was silent. So silent. There were no other cars or people around for as far as the eye could see. The welcoming white church looked as if it belonged on a postcard. It was surrounded by green fields of ripening corn stalks, but the church itself was on a small, well-cared-for plot of freshly mowed grass. It had beautiful flowers of pink, white and yellow planted below the welcome sign next to the front steps. The air was impeccably warm, with the slightest of perfect breezes. The enormous blue sky with its cotton-ball clouds seemed to go on forever. The sound of buzzing insects and of our footsteps crunching upon the gravel road was all that could be heard.

The woman meeting us was running late, so I walked the grounds to take it all in and to take some photos. There was a small white building directly across from the church on the other side of the gravel road. It looked as if it were a one-room schoolhouse back in the day and was now being used for storage. When the woman arrived a few minutes later she introduced herself as Cheryl Doe, and said she was the church secretary. She asked who my ancestor was that I was researching. I told her Reverend Lars Green. She lit up and said she believed his photo was downstairs.

She began her tour, and I marveled at being in the actual building where Grandpa Rolf's great-uncle had spent so many hours writing sermons, preaching, teaching, and caring for his flock throughout the decades. My eyes were viewing the exact sights his had viewed all those years ago. My grandpa's uncles, his father's brothers, had stood upon that very ground, after driving their wagons from their homesteads to church.

I was eager to see more. While Cheryl and Sandy chatted in the back of the sanctuary about who they knew in common, the way Minnesotans seem to do, I took a seat in one of the front pews. I took it all in: the ornate woodwork on the pews, the expansive ceiling, the simplicity of its design, and the enveloping comfort of its walls. I bowed my head and said a prayer of thankfulness. I gave thanks for merely being there, right then, in that moment. When I opened my eyes and looked up the first thing I noticed was the large stained-glass window behind the pulpit at the front of the church. I stood up to take a closer look. Engraved within the bottom of the beautiful window, patterned in red, green and yellow it read," L. E. Green." I smiled. It was all too perfect.

Lake Hanska Lutheran Church & Close-up of Stained Glass in Background
Photo Credit: Author's Personal Collection.

As I was leaving the sanctuary, Cheryl invited me to sign the guest book. As I was signing, Sandy shared that I had lived in Hanska

130

fifteen years ago and was visiting for the first time since. Cheryl told us that she used to live in Hanska as well, years ago on Viking Avenue. I stopped writing. I looked at her.

"I lived on Viking Avenue," I said. "206 Viking Avenue."

We both stood in amazement as we realized that the church secretary of Lake Hanska Lutheran Church, the church I had only recently learned about and that was established by Grandpa Rolf's great-uncle, was the woman we bought our house from when we moved from Poulsbo to Hanska fifteen years earlier. It was yet another remarkable, unbelievable coincidence.

"You bought my house?!" she asked incredulously.

We talked about the shed that had a huge smiley face painted on the back. It had faced the corn field, and was the first thing we would see when we drove the back way home. The boys would excitedly announce "There's the smiley face!" the moment it came into view. That quirky, whimsical painting with its bright yellow smile had welcomed us home so many times. Cheryl told me that she was the one who had painted it. For as long as my family lives, we'll always remember the huge smiley face painted on the shed of our little house on the prairie.

I was feeling full of excitement and electricity when Sandy and I bade our farewells to Cheryl and exchanged our contact information with her. We continued on our journey to the other two churches on the schedule that afternoon: Linden Lutheran a few miles away, and Our Saviors Lutheran in Butternut. The fourth of the churches, Trinity Lutheran in Madelia, I planned to visit on the way out of town the next morning with Noah.

Within no time at all we were at Linden Lutheran Church. Like Lake Hanska Lutheran, Linden was painted white, and built in the late 1800s Protestant style. It was clearly being well cared for by volunteers. An old metal gate surrounded the small cemetery that was a few yards from the church entrance. I opened the gate while Sandy checked the plot guide in a large metal box in front of the cemetery. But I didn't need any help. The first grave I saw after I opened the metal gate belonged to Bernhard Green. Bernhard had made the voyage across the ocean when he was just a small boy.

His final resting place was under a beautiful shade tree, a peaceful respite from the beating sun. Next to Bernhard's stone were his daughters Cora and Ada. I took a few steps away and looked upwards toward the expanse of blue sky. My eyes fell to the tall, pointed spire of the church. Atop its most heavenward point was a thin cross, and upon that thin cross sat a small bird. Watching us, welcoming us.

Bird atop Linden Lutheran spire. Photo Credit: Author's Personal Collection.

Our last stop of the evening was to Our Savior's Lutheran Church in the village of Butternut. It was the third of the five churches Reverend Green was pastor to, but unlike the old, prairie-style churches of Lake Hanska Lutheran and Linden Lutheran, this one was modernized, made of red brick, and didn't have a cemetery. The original pioneer church had been demolished and rebuilt decades earlier.

My final destination while in Minnesota was to visit the grave of Reverend Lars Engebretsen Green. The following morning, Noah and I made our trip to Trinity Lutheran Church in Madelia. The town, while very small, was significantly larger than Hanska. It was late morning and the summer weather was comfortably warm and dry.

Trinity Lutheran was closed. The parking lot was empty and no one was in sight. I walked the cement path towards the main entrance, and as I did so I held the black iron railing wondering if Uncle Lars had held this same railing as he walked this path countless times (I later learned that this was not the original Trinity Lutheran, but like Butternut it had been rebuilt after Reverend Green's passing). I peered into the window. The building was still and dark and peaceful. I quietly placed my hand on the trunk of a large maple tree. I plucked a low-hanging leaf to bring home with me, and we continued down the road to the cemetery.

There was no need for us to use the cemetery directory. The large, granite monument was immediately seen as the cemetery came into view. We were alone. We parked the car and made our way towards the tall monument. The white stone was lovingly engraved, and had a classic yet elegant design. It pointed toward the heavens. Noah and I took a moment to quietly give our respect, and he took photos so I could remember this time always. Directly behind the monument was Reverend Green's beloved wife Jensine and their seven daughters, four of whom he lost as small children. In my heart I spoke to Lars. I told him that it had been an absolute pleasure and honor getting to learn about the fascinating lives he and his family, my family, lived while settling the prairie. And once again, I gave thanks for allowing me be right there, in that moment.

On Zion Lutheran Church's website, I was moved by a prayer that I read in their welcome. I found it perfectly fitting to my journey of discovery:

O God, you have called your servants to ventures of which we cannot see the ending, by paths as yet untrodden, through perils unknown. Give us faith to go out with good courage, not knowing where we go, but only that your hand is leading us and your love supporting us; through Jesus Christ our Lord. Amen.

Paying respects at Reverend Lars Green's Monument. July 2022
Photo Credit: Author's Personal Collection.

The Churches

Jens Harbo Farm, First Meeting Location of Linden Lutheran
Photo Credit: Unknown.

*L*inden Lutheran Church was the first Norwegian Lutheran church in Brown County, Minnesota. The Harbo, Thormodson, Omsrud, and Paulson families were among the first immigrants to settle in the area. They were from the Stavanger area of Norway, and had originally settled in Rock Prairie, Wisconsin, before relocating to Brown County. The church was built on the farm of Jens Harbo in the summer of 1859. Being the first Norwegian Lutheran Church in the area, it served a very large area of settlers.

Leading that first service on the farm was an unconventional pastor. His name was Anders Emil Frederickson, but he was known throughout the area as "Buckskin" due to his unusual attire. Buckskin was a student of theology in Norway, but was unable to become ordained in America. Instead, he served his faith by helping newly formed Norwegian communities build churches for their congregations. The Norwegian settlers from Butternut Valley, Madelia, Riverdale, and Lake Hanska had all belonged to the Linden congregation before breaking off. In 1869, farmers in Butternut and Lake Hanska left the congregation to build churches closer to their farms so it wouldn't be such a long journey on Sundays.

The following article was written by local historian Joel Botten for the Friends of Linden's *Limelights* newsletter in November 2022. It has been included with permission.

Linden Lutheran church was founded at the home of Jens and Cecelia Harbo on July 2, 1859, 163 years ago. Local Norwegian pioneers, who lived near Madelia (city founded in 1857) decided to form the Rosendale congregation on the same day as Linden in 1859. Linden has claimed to be first.

The Linden congregation continued to worship in homes until a log schoolhouse was built on the north-east corner of Jens Harbo's land. The school was used for worship until 1869 when it was proposed to build a separate church. Disagreement on a site ensued. Concern centered on the distance families had to travel to church, spend 2 or 3 hours there and have time to get home to do chores, etc. Seven to ten miles was the railroad's distance between stations and the distance an ox and wagon could usually make a round trip in one day. Oxen traveled about two miles per hour.

Butternut (1869) and Lake Hanska (1869) left the Linden congregation to build churches in their immediate vicinity. In 1873, just three years after the founding of Lake Hanska, members from Albin township left to establish Albion Lutheran church. A discontented group left Lake Hanska in 1881 to found the Nora Unitarian Universalist congregation. In1903–1904 Lake Hanska members helped to establish Zion Lutheran church in the village of Hanska. (The city was incorporated in 1901.) Danish families founded Rice Lake church in1872, so nationality may also have played a role in their decision.

Our Saviors Lutheran church of Butternut recently closed and chose to donate their history and memorabilia to the Linden Lutheran church thereby, they "returned" to Linden. Rice Lake Lutheran also "returned" as its altar painting had been displayed in the Butternut church after Rice Lake closed in 1963.The painting now hangs in Linden church. Thanks to an active cemetery association and faithful Friends of Linden group, the Linden church is preserved, and the cemetery maintained. Each Memorial Day weekend Linden is open for visitors. — Joel Botten

Linden Lutheran Church, 2024. Photo Credit: Author's Personal Collection.

According to Lake Hanska Lutheran's archival records, the first services for the church were held under a large oak tree on Thor Omsrud's farm in 1859. People came by ox and wagon from miles away to attend. Ten years later, after the church broke away from Linden Lutheran, their constitution was written on November 9, 1869. The territory it served was vast, and included the townships of Lake Hanska, Albin, and part of Nelson.

Lake Hanska Lutheran. 2024. Photo Credit: Author's Personal Collection.

The Albion Norwegian Lutheran congregation in St. James, in Watonwan County, consisted of 148 members was organized in 1871 by Reverend Hattrem. The first church building was constructed in 1885, but it was struck by lightning in 1908, and was rebuilt that same year.

Trinity Lutheran Church was established on October 28, 1870, as the Norwegian Evangelical Lutheran Trinity Church in Madelia, Minnesota. Reverend Thor Hattrem was also its founding pastor as well. The construction of the church building began in 1878, and it was officially dedicated after its completion ten years later in 1888. The brick building that is the church today was constructed in 1951.

Trinity Lutheran Church. Date Unknown.
Photo Credit: Watonwan County Historical Society.

Those early decades of pioneer life for the Norwegian settlers were extremely difficult—too difficult for those of us in the twenty-first century to fully comprehend. The pioneering members of the congregations suffered extreme poverty, blistering heat, freezing cold temperatures, crop failures, fires, sickness and early death. Dugouts and log cabins were the people's first residences. Ole Reinert of Butterfield wrote of his remembrances of those days, "As old and as forgetful as I am, I can never forget what we went through in the first years we were on these prairies. One can guess at the long trips we had with oxen—with no roads or bridges—in rain and snow storms. If there had not remained a bit of Viking blood in our veins, the hardships would have been unendurable."

The congregations of St. Olaf, Butterfield, Long Lake, Albion, and Rosendale were all combined into one, having the same pastor and same parsonage. Rosendale Lutheran is the oldest Lutheran church in Watonwan County. The first pastor to serve the congregation was Reverend Anders Friederichson, who led the people from 1859 to1863. The church was without a pastor for eight years before Reverend Hattrem started to serve Rosendale as well in

1871. He passed away on January 10, 1873, and is buried in the Linden Lutheran cemetery. The search for a new pastor immediately began. No one would have guessed at the time that the pastor who took his place would become one of the longest-serving pastors in the area's history.

Zion Lutheran Church, Hanska, MN. Photo Credit: www.prairielandlutheran.org

The Green Immigrants

Once the European immigrants to America were settled and established on their homesteads, it was extremely common for them to pave the way for family and friends to join them. Letters were written home telling about the journey in great detail—what they encountered, tips for a successful voyage, places to go for help, places to avoid, and most importantly, if where they had settled was a good place to plant roots. Whether to stay in Norway or take a chance in America was the most significant, life-altering decision to make. It was a long and difficult journey, of which every detail had to be considered carefully.

In Norway, only a small percentage of the people were landowners. Land was a type of wealth only attainable by the highest class. Many Norwegian men knew they would never own their own property due to the systems in place, so when free land became available in the U.S. under the American Homestead Act of 1862, thousands jumped at the opportunity.

Reverend Lars Green, the first of his family to arrive in America, helped bring a dozen of his family members to Minnesota after he was settled: three of his siblings, and nine nieces and nephews. Some stayed and lived their entire lives in the area, and are buried locally. Others stayed only briefly before heading elsewhere—northern Minnesota, Wisconsin, Manitoba, and the Pacific Northwest. All were provided a safe spot to land after arriving from their long journey across the sea. With Reverend Green's help, they were given a place to gather their bearings in Hanska–Madelia before venturing out to forge their destinies. Thousands of Americans can trace their lineage back to this handful of Green family members from the Grinkelsrud Farm in Nes, Akershus, Norway.

The following chapter was written with members of the Green Family in mind—those who are interested in family genealogy. It will also be of interest to local historians, families who have remained in Hanska for generations, and anyone who is fascinated by the American pioneering experience—especially those who came from Norway during the late nineteenth century. Every immigrant has an

141

amazing story. These are the brief stories of twelve family members who risked everything they had for a chance at the American Dream.

REVEREND LARS GREEN'S FAMILY TREE

Father, Embret Olsen Nordgarn Grinkelsrud 1802–1877
Mother, Barbro Nilsdatter Svangerud   1812–1893

Their Children:

1. Ole Nicolai, born 1833 – stayed in Norway
2. Bernt Sigvart, born 1834 (the author's second great-grandfather) – stayed in Norway
   a. **Axel, born 1861 – immigrated to America in 1881**
   b. **Emma, born 1863 – immigrated to America in 1883**
   c. **Gina, born 1865 – immigrated solo in 1880 at age 14**
   d. **Lars, born 1867 – immigrated to America in 1883 at age 16**
   e. Bernt, born 1869 – stayed in Norway
3. Berthe Marie, born 1837 – stayed in Norway
4. **Lars Engebretsen, born 1841 – immigrated to America 1866**
5. **(twin) Karen, born 1844 – immigrated to America in 1881**
6. (twin) Edda Birgitte, born 1844 – stayed in Norway
7. **Gustav Engebretsen, born 1846 – immigrated to America in 1881**
   a. **Clara, born 1870 – immigrated to America 1881**
   b. **Frithjof, born 1872 – immigrated to America 1881**
   c. **Bernhard, born 1873 – immigrated to America 1881**
   d. **Olaf, born 1875 – immigrated to America 1881**
   e. **Karl, born 1880 – immigrated to America 1881**
8. **Maren "Olava," born 1849 – immigrated to America in 1881**
9. Ida Birgitte born 1851 – stayed in Norway
10. Berte Kristine born 1854 – stayed in Norway

Lars E. Green's Parents

Embret Olsen Nordgarn Grinkelsrud and Barbro Nilsdatter
1802 - 1877   1812 – 1893

Nikolai Grinkelsrud.

Ole Nikolai Grinkelsrud
1833- 1922
1st Son of Embret and Barbro

Bernt Sigvart Engebretsen Green
1834 - 1905
2nd Son of Embret and Barbro
Author's Great-Great Grandfather

Gustav Green
Reverend Green's Brother, Grandpa Rolf's Great-Uncle
Born July 15, 1846

Gustav Green. Possibly 1868 wedding photo.

Reverend Green's brother Gustav immigrated to Hanska, Minnesota in 1881. Gustav Engebretsen Green was five years younger than Lars, and was the youngest of the four Grinkelsrud brothers. He had the most adventurous character of all the siblings who immigrated, and his story is the most tragic.

He was born during the height of summer at the family estate. Being the last of four sons, he knew he was not to inherit Grinkelsrud, but as a result of his father's higher social class, he had privileges that most Norwegians at the time did not.

In the Norway of the mid-to-late nineteenth century, a man's social status was indicated by his profession. Skilled craftsmanship was highly regarded. As a young man, Gustav became a master-level baker and moved to Oslo, where the residents were generally wealthier than the majority of the country's rural population.

On March 30, 1868, Gustav married Fredrikke Fredriksdatter at Trinity Church (Trefoldighetskirken) in Oslo. Their son Fridtjof Emil was the first child of their union. He was born on February 19, 1869, but sadly the infant did not live long. He died nine days after his birth. According to church records, he was baptized at home on the day he was born. Gustav and Fredrikke had called for a priest to come quickly, thinking the baby wouldn't survive the day. He did, however, live another eight days before passing on February 28, 1869. His cause of death is listed as "complications from eclampsia."

In his 2018 article examining Norwegian church-registry deaths and infant mortality, H. L. Sommerseth wrote: "Among infants, we find that 20 percent of all infant deaths were registered with konvulsioner/kramper/eclampsia as the main cause of death." During that time, "eclampsia" was a broadly used term for convulsions and failure to thrive in infants. Little Fridtjof Emil was among those twenty percent, and was buried in the Vår Felsers Cemetery.

Vår Felsers translates to "Our Savior's." It was, and still is, the main church of the Church of Norway, and is located in downtown Oslo. Fridtjof's burial was another indication of Gustav's social standing. At the time, only the affluent could afford to buy burial plots in that cemetery. Vår Felsers is now known as the Oslo Cathedral. It's where the country's most notable citizens of history are buried, including the painter Edvard Munch and the playwright Henrik Ibsen.

It wasn't long after Fridtjof's burial that the couple was blessed with another pregnancy. Their second child Clara Betsy was born on January 6, 1870, and baptized a month later at Vår Felsers. Clara's birth was followed by the arrivals of four sons: Frithjof Emil in 1871 (named after his brother Fridtjof Emil who passed prior), Bernhard Gotfried in 1873, Olaf Nicolai in 1875, and Carl Ludwig in 1877. The family lived at Tejeng 24 in Oslo/Christiana.

Unfortunately, Gustav and Fredrikke lost little Carl Ludwig two months after he was born. To add to the dreadful sorrow, Fredrikke died only a few weeks after the baby's funeral, on September 6, 1877. Burial records show her cause of death was tuberculosis. Gustav's terrible year of loss was not yet done, however. On December 3, 1877, his father Embret died as well. In just three months' time, Gustav had tragically lost his wife, his child, and his father.

Fredrikke Green

Fredrikke's passing left Gustav a widower with four young children to care for—all of whom were under the age of seven. He found comfort in a neighbor woman, Andrea Jacobsdatter, from Lier. Andrea was herself a widow, and had also experienced great loss. Both her husband and young son had recently passed, and she was mourning just as Gustav was. Exactly three years and one day after little Carl's death, another son was born to Gustav. Using the renaming custom of the time, he named the new baby Karl Elvin in honor of his lost child, Carl Ludwig. Two months after their son was born, Gustav and Andrea were married on September 5, 1880, at Østre Aker Church. Plans were soon set in motion to start a new life in America.

On March 30, 1881, six months after their wedding, the newly blended family set sail aboard the *Angelo* to join Gustav's brother Lars in Madelia, Minnesota. The departure date would have been Gustav and Fredrikke's twelfth wedding anniversary. As the ship moved away from the pier, and the Oslo landscape slowly disappeared from view, Gustav silently bade farewell to his two infant sons and his first wife. He tucked them fondly, and deeply, into his heart forever.

Baby Karl was eight months old when they left Norway. Andrea undoubtedly had her hands full managing four young children, plus an infant, during the long, crowded voyage. Clara, being the eldest daughter at eleven years old, likely unburdened much of the responsibility and care for her four younger brothers.

Gustav, Andrea, and the children weren't the only members of the Green family on board the *Angelo* that morning. The party consisted of ten relatives in total. Gustav and Reverend Green's two sisters Karen, age thirty-seven, and Olava, age thirty-one, joined the family as they journeyed across the ocean to Minnesota. Also joining them was Gustav and Reverend Green's twenty-year-old nephew, Axel. Gustav relied on his young nephew to assist him in protecting the three women and five children during the arduous journey.

Their arrival to New York City preceded the Statue of Liberty, whose sight welcomed immigrants from around the world beginning in 1892. From New York, the family traveled by steamship up the Huron River to Albany, then to Buffalo, then to Milwaukee on the Great Lakes. Passenger lists show that the Green family travelled to La Crosse, Wisconsin from Milwaukee. From La Crosse they took a train to Minneapolis, then connected to the train to New Ulm. The Hanska township's train station was not yet in operation, and it's not difficult to imagine Reverend Green meeting the family in New Ulm with an extra wagon to carry all his relatives and their belongings.

Lars Green hadn't seen his siblings in over fifteen years when they were all reunited on the Minnesota prairie in the summer of 1881. Axel, now a young man, was a five-year-old boy when Lars left for America. On that early June day in New Ulm, Reverend Green met his five nieces and nephews for the very first time. It was surely a wonderful reunion for all involved, and much news of friends and family back home was undoubtedly shared. The reverend brought his exhausted family back to his farm in Madelia to gather and rest while they made plans for their futures.

About a month later, on July 2, 1881, Gustav purchased a 78.5-acre homestead in Hanska, eight miles from his brother's farm. He immediately got to work farming. The current address of where Reverend Green's farm was located is 28557 State Highway 15 in Madelia. The coordinates of Gustav's land were: Township 108, Range 31, Section 24, subsection of sections NE ¼ of SE ¼ and Government Lot 2. Looking at a modern map of Hanska, the northern half of his land would have been from the corner of Broadway and 2nd St./Main St. east to what was once the edge of Ouren Lake, but is now a large field. The property then extends many acres southward, towards modern day Highway 257. Today, the highway acts as a marker which divides the entirety of his property in half. The following image from Brown County archives highlights Gustav's original homestead.

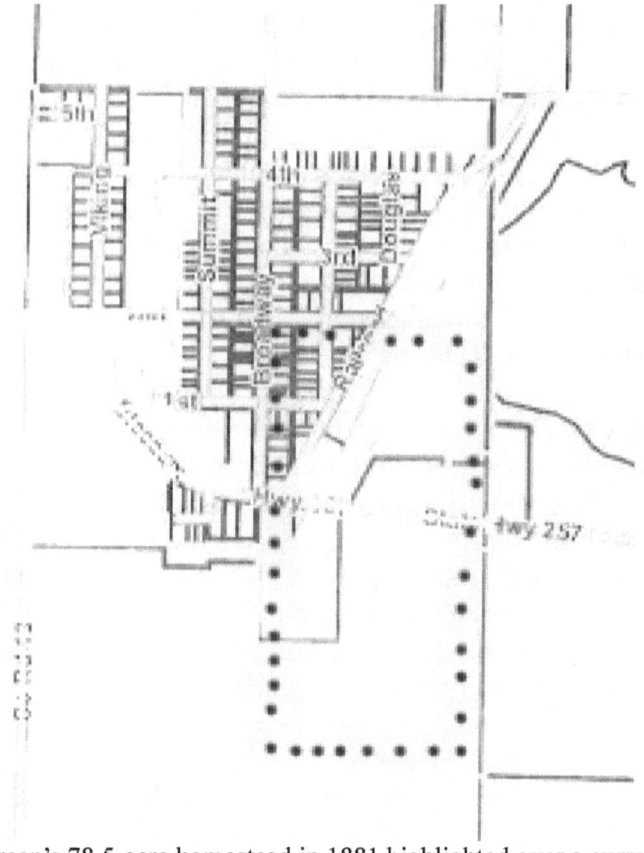

Gustav Green's 78.5-acre homestead in 1881 highlighted over a current map of Hanska, MN.

Once they were settled on their homestead, Gustav and Andrea's second child Sigri Amelie was born on May 4, 1882. She was baptized by her uncle Lars on August 20, 1882, at Lake Hanska Lutheran Church. Sadly, she died one month to the day after her baptism. She was the third infant Gustav had buried, and the second child lost to Andrea as well. Andrea and Gustav's third child Gina Amalie was born October 3, 1883. Unfortunately, the day could not be celebrated. Tragically, Andrea died giving birth to baby Gina. Once again, the devastated Gustav was left a widower, with six children to care for including a newborn. And once again, young Clara at thirteen years old became the main caregiver to her younger siblings while their father worked the fields.

Gustav's misfortunes were not over. Baby Gina died a few weeks before her first birthday on September 20, 1884. In a cruel coincidence, the date was the exact anniversary of her sister Sigri's passing two years prior, and the baby girl died five days after Reverend Green lost his own infant daughter as well. For unknown reasons, there are no Minnesota cemetery records of Andrea, Sigri or Gina. However, Brown County birth, baptism, and death records confirm the existence of their short lives. As was all too common at the time, there was so much loss of young life within the Green family of Madelia and Hanska during the 1880s.

Two years after the string of tragedies, the 1885 Minnesota State Census shows Gustav and his children still homesteading in Lake Hanska that May. His nephew Axel, then twenty-four years old, was living with the family as well, working the farm with Gustav and his sons. Frithjof was almost fourteen, Bernhard was eleven, and Olaf was ten. The boys helped their father and Axel as much as they could with the intense farm work while Clara made the meals, kept the home and looked after five-year-old Karl.

Illegitimate births were not socially accepted in the nineteenth century in either Norwegian or American cultures, but as history repeatedly shows us, they did happen. Another event often considered taboo within a family tree was marriage between first cousins. Both of these situations happened within the Green family when Gustav's daughter Clara and his nephew Axel were married by a Justice of the Peace on June 20,1885, in New Ulm, Minnesota. Axel was twenty years old when he accompanied eleven-year-old Clara and her family across the Atlantic. She was barely fifteen when she became pregnant, and was four months along in her pregnancy at their wedding.

Shortly after signing away his daughter, Gustav made plans to leave Minnesota and travel back home to Norway. He sold his homestead to his sister Karen and her husband Ellef Asleson on November 10, 1885. Gustav decided to bring five-year-old Carl with him on the winter journey overseas, but left his three older sons behind to be looked after by Clara, family, and community friends. When Clara and Axel left Lake Hanska to start anew in Wisconsin in 1886, her three little brothers were scattered to surrounding farms.

Immediately after arriving home to his farm in Skedmo, Akershus, Norway, Gustav married for a third time on January 30, 1886 to Karoline Olsen in Vestre Aker. Because the marriage occurred so quickly after he arrived, arrangements had likely been made in advance via correspondence while Gustav was still in Minnesota.

Nine months after the wedding, their son Ingvald Karsten was born. The births of three daughters followed in rapid succession— Sofie in 1888, Gulborg in 1889, and Helga in 1890. Young Carl, whose mother and sisters had died in Minnesota, was placed at least temporarily in the foster care of an elderly neighboring couple in Norway. He was listed twice in the 1891 Norway Census: first in one household with his father, stepmother, and four half-siblings; the second time with the elderly couple as "foster son."

This leaves much room for speculation. Perhaps Gustav's new wife didn't appreciate or care for the boy. Perhaps one of their three small children was ill with a dangerous childhood disease, and Carl was being protected. Or, perhaps the elderly couple needed farm assistance. The reason why is unknown, but money was not a factor. Gustav was a landowner and master baker, according to the 1891 Census, and had four servants living in the household.

With his affairs in order and matters settled, Gustav booked passage for himself, Caroline, and the five children back to America on March 18, 1893. Gustav likely knew when he departed the harbor shores that morning that he would never see Norway or his family again. His mother Barbro died on April 4, 1893, two weeks after her youngest son steamed towards America for the second time. At the time of their departure, Caroline was heavily pregnant. Five days into the journey, her and Gustav's son Thoralf was born at sea during the Atlantic crossing back to Minnesota.

The newly opened Ellis Island had been welcoming immigrants for only a year when Gustav returned. Unlike his arrival with his first family in 1881, they were welcomed this time by the sight of the iconic Statue of Liberty as they entered New York Harbor. It was his wife Caroline and their children's first time stepping foot on American soil, and young Carl's second. Being five years old when he left the first time, he remembered the big city and the people and prairie back home. After being processed through New York, the family began the long journey back to Hanska. Karen and Ellef rented the homestead that was once Gustav's back to him.

The 1895 Minnesota Census shows Gustav and his family farming in Hanska. Although he signed a five-year rental agreement with his sister and brother-in-law when he returned, he left Hanska for the last time three years later in 1896. He left the care of the farm to his grown sons when he decided to move his new family to the northern part of the state.

Discouraged by renting and desiring land of his own, Gustav sought opportunities outside of Brown County. Taking full advantage of the one hundred and sixty acres offered by the Homestead Act of 1862, Gustav moved north where new townships were being developed in Roseau County. The 375-mile journey took the family three to four weeks to travel by wagon, perhaps longer since all six children were under the age of eight. The couple chose Hereim Township, approximately fifty-five miles from the Canadian border, for their fresh start. The homestead was located about three miles west of Greenbush, Minnesota, and was unnamed at the time of their arrival, then known only as Township 160.

Gustav and Caroline arrived to the Greenbush area four years prior to a mass influx of German, Polish, and Scandinavian immigrants in 1900. Unlike Hanska and Madelia, whose residents were primarily Norwegian, the Greenbush area was more diverse. When Gustav and the family arrived, there was very little to call a town. The first general store wouldn't be built until two years later in 1898. In 1904, the arrival of the railroad put Greenbush on the map. The stores in the "old" part of town all moved their locations to "new" Greenbush to be near the railroad.

Gustav had finally set down roots. He and Caroline lived the remainder of their years on their homestead in Hereim with their large family. Amazingly, Caroline would have another seven children, all sons, after the family arrived to Minnesota. In total, she gave Gustav nine sons and three daughters, for a total of twenty-one children fathered in his lifetime. The couple also adopted a baby girl, Julia Thompson (McCelain), when she was three weeks old after her mother died.

The Norwegian censuses show Gustav and his brothers as "landhandlers" with servants. This contrasts with his life in Minnesota. Gustav wore two hats during his lifetime—one of a landowning master tradesman with servants when at home in Norway, the other of a rugged immigrant farmer homesteading his land in Minnesota.

The 1900 U.S. Census states that Gustav became a naturalized citizen, but he did not speak English. This could have been a mistake on the part of the census taker, but perhaps Norwegian was in fact his only language ever spoken.

Gustav's life journey ended on January 31, 1916, in Roseau County, the day after he and Caroline celebrated their thirtieth wedding anniversary. He was sixty-nine years old. He is buried in Bethania Free Lutheran Cemetery in Greenbush, Minnesota. Caroline would live another twenty-seven years after Gustav's passing. She died in 1943, and is buried beside her beloved husband. The four-foot pillar monument that marks Gustav's grave has the incorrect year of birth engraved on it, reading 1848 instead of the true year he was born, 1846.

The Greenbush, MN Centennial Book (1905–2005) written by the Greenbush Centennial Committee is posted on the City of Greenbush website. There's a section in the book about the early pioneers of Greenbush, and Gustav is included. It discusses his love of baking, and how his family carried fond memories of his delicious Christmas specialty, julekake. It also wrote of Caroline's love for homemaking, and visiting and conversing with friends and family in her later years.

The chapter on pioneers also details a terrible fire that nearly ruined Gustav's homestead and legacy a few years after he passed away:

In 1919 or 1920 a terrible fire burned the homestead down leaving only one granary standing. They were finishing the fall threshing. It was a hot day with a strong sourtherly wind and the blower box on the threshing machine became over heated and started the fire. The house, barn, summer kitchen, blacksmith shop and another granary burned. A house was moved in for the winter and the farmstead was rebuilt the following spring.

Gustav Engebretsen Green lived an amazing life of hard work, tragedy, and resilience. He was the embodiment of the American Dream. He had a true pioneering spirit of strength and fortitude that's difficult for generations that came after him to fully comprehend. When his eyes closed for the last time during the winter of 1916, they closed upon a chapter of American history that can never be repeated.

Caroline and Gustav Green 1915.
Last photo taken of Gustav before his passing in 1916.
Photo Credit: *The Greenbush, MN Centennial Book 1905–2005* and Albin and Muriel Green.

Gustav's Children

Gustav Green (widower) and his children circa 1879. Norway.
From left to right: Bernhard, Gustav, Olaf, Frithjof, Clara.

Clara Betsy Green
Gustav Green's Daughter, Reverend Green's Niece
Born January 6, 1870
&
Axel Emil Green
Gustav & Reverend Green's Nephew, Grandpa Rolf's Uncle
Born February 24, 1861

Axel, Clara and baby Gunda Green circa 1887, Wisconsin.

Gustav's first child to survive infancy was his daughter Clara Betsy. She was born on January 6, 1870, to Gustav and his first wife Fredrikke, less than a year after the passing of the couple's first child, Fridtjof Emil. Like her brother, Clara was baptized at the prominent Vår Felsers Church, known today as the Oslo Cathedral.

The 1875 Norway Census shows young Clara and her three younger brothers living in Øien nordre, Østfold, Norway, with their mother and family maid. Beside Fredrikke's name is the note "Baker Green's wife." The family was somehow listed twice by the census. One possibility is that the family may have relocated and traveled between the two localities during the census taking. The census also shows the family living at Tøiengade 24 in Oslo. Her father is listed as a "Bagermester," which translates to "master baker."

Axel Emil Green was born on February 24, 1861 in Lystad, and was baptized at Sørem Parish, which is now within the Lillestrøm municipality of Akershus County. Axel's parents were Bernt and Gunda Green. Bernt was the older brother of Gustav and Reverend Green. Bernt and Ole, the two oldest brothers of the Grinkelsrud family, stayed behind in Norway and never immigrated. Gustav and Lars, the two youngest brothers, left to create their lives in America.

Bernt is the 2x great-grandfather of the author of this book. Axel is the uncle of my ninety-three-year-old grandfather, his father's brother. It's amazing how the generations really aren't that long ago.

When Axel was twenty years old, he decided that, like his uncles, his future was destined for America. On the *Angelo* passenger list, he wrote that he was from Mødum, and that he was heading to Madelia, Minnesota. Together with his aunts Karen and Olava, his uncle Gustav, Gustav's wife Andrea, and their five children, the extended family set out for the voyage to America.

Clara was seven years old when her mother died, and eleven when she immigrated to America with her family. She was called "Betsy" by close friends and family. As the eldest daughter she was vital in the caretaking of her four little brothers during the voyage and the difficult days of the overland journey, as well as the early homesteading days. Clara was there for the death of her stepmother Andrea, as well as the tragic passing of her two infant half-sisters while living in Hanska.

When she was fifteen, the 1885 Minnesota state census took place. It shows widower Gustav and his children homesteading in Hanska. Axel lived with the family as well, and helped Gustav and the younger boys with the farm work.

It's difficult to imagine and fully understand the hardships young Clara endured, and the choices that were made for her by the men in her life. With a world of responsibility on her shoulders, she found herself pregnant at age fifteen by her adult cousin Axel. It was decided that she and Axel would marry. The two were married by a Justice of the Peace on June 20, 1885, in New Ulm, Minnesota. Her uncle Reverend Lars did not approve of the cousins' union, and therefore would not marry them in the Lutheran church. Because Clara was a minor, her father Gustav had to sign his parental consent on the bottom of the marriage record. Axel also signed, affirming that he and Clara were not related by blood. Four months to the day after their wedding, Clara and Axel's first child was born on October 20, 1885.

They named their baby daughter Gunda Fredrikke—Gunda after Axel's mother, and Fredrikke after Clara's mother. Little Gunda was baptized by Reverend Green at Lake Hanska Lutheran Church on New Year's Day, 1886. Shortly after little Gunda's baptism, the young family left for Cedar Falls in Dunn County, Wisconsin. They stayed a few years in Cedar Falls before settling in Ashland, Wisconsin, where they remained for the rest of their lives. After moving to Ashland, Axel gave up farming and began a long career working as a brakeman and repairman for the Chicago & Northwestern Railroad Company. He was a longtime member of the Ashland Sons of Norway organization.

In the 1900 Census, they were renting a house at 122 6th Street in Ashland, but according to the 1910 census they purchased their own home at 1102 5th Avenue East. Sometime within the first decade of the twentieth century they were able to purchase their own home.

In 1910, Clara stated on the census that she had thirteen children, eleven of whom were living.

Axel died the week before Christmas in 1918, at the age of fifty-seven. His passing left Clara a widow just shy of her forty-eighth birthday, with sixteen children to care for. The youngest was just two years old. The 1920 census shows Clara owning the home free and clear with no mortgage, which was surely a blessing for the large family, knowing they would always have a roof over their heads.

The 1940 Census shows all of the children had moved away from the home except for daughter Ida, who is listed as "head" of the family. Ida was an unmarried school teacher. She and Clara lived together in the house on 5th Avenue until Clara's passing on June 11, 1957. Like many women of her generation, she lived a long, difficult life of eighty-seven years. She was pregnant or nursing from the age of fifteen to forty-seven. She and Axel had eighteen children total, sixteen of whom survived into adulthood. The couple is buried together at Mount Hope Cemetery in Ashland, Wisconsin.

Axel Green, circa 1881, age 20. Norway.

Older Clara "Betsy" Green, Date Unknown.

Frithjof Emil Green
Gustav's First Son, Reverend Green's Nephew
Born May 23, 1871

Gustav's four oldest sons, the ones who arrived with their father and stepmother in 1881, all remained in the area, at least for a while. His eldest son Frithjof Emil was six years old when his mother died, and was nine when he landed in America. As was the Norwegian tradition, he was named after his brother, the first Fridtjof Emil, who died at one week old in 1869. The spelling difference of their first names distinguishes the two.

Being the oldest son, the boy was likely given much responsibility by his father. After Frithjof's stepmother Andrea and his two little half-sisters passed away, and his oldest sister Clara left for Wisconsin after her marriage, Frithjof was fifteen years old when his father left Minnesota for Norway to visit family, tend to business affairs, and find a new wife.

It's not known which farm Frithjof was originally sent to work at after his father left. But in the late 1890s he was working as a farmhand on widower Jens Anderson's farm in Linden. Like the Green family, Jens was also from Akershus County. His second wife was Karen Klovstad, a recent immigrant who moved to Linden in June 1897. Jens and Karen were married on July 21, 1897, a month after she arrived. Karen was also a widow, and based on the short time between her arrival and marriage, it was likely an arranged union.

Karen immigrated with her twenty-one-year-old daughter Julia Klovstad. Frithjof and Julia soon fell in love during their days on the farm, and the two were married on June 6, 1900, at Trinity Lutheran Church in Madelia. Frithjof asked his Uncle Lars to perform the marriage, and the reverend once again officiated the holy union for one of his relatives. Frithjof's younger brother Olaf signed as witness during the ceremony. It was a very busy month of celebration for the Green family. Lars married Frithjof's brother Bernhard in June of 1900 as well.

The 1900 Census taker visited Linden a week after the newlyweds were married. Frithjof was listed as "boarder" on the Jens Anderson farm, and Julia as "wife." Their marriage would unfortunately be brief. Frithjof and Julia's son was born on February 25, 1901, but tragically young Julia died from complications from the birth twelve days after delivering her son. The baby was named Juel Martin in honor of his mother who died giving him life.

Based on census records, it can be assumed that his grandparents, Karen and Jens, took baby Juel immediately after Julia died and raised him from a newborn. In 1902, when Juel was a year old, his grandparents retired from farming, and Jens bought a city lot in Hanska to build a home.

Mourning the death of his beloved wife and unable to care for his son, Frithjof left the area. The 1905 Minnesota Census shows him working as a miller in Camp Release Township in Lac qui Parle County, Minnesota. At that time, Juel was living with his grandparents at 100 Summit Avenue in Hanska, as he was for the 1910 Census as well. Also living on Summit Avenue was Frithjof's brother Olaf. Juel grew up with an uncle and cousins to play with who lived a few houses down the street, but his relationship with his father Frithjof during his childhood is unknown.

100 Summit Ave. Hanska, MN
Photo Credit: Author's Personal Collection.

In an interesting mystery, Karen and Jens used the last name "Bekken" in the 1905 and 1910 Censuses. Jens' brother, sister, stepchildren, and daughter Clara used Anderson and Bekken interchangeably throughout their lives. The reason why is not known for certain.

The New Ulm Review posted the class list of the ten graduating seniors from Hanska High School on June 9, 1915. Fifteen-year-old Juel was among them. The celebratory season came to an end two weeks later when Juel's grandmother Karen, who had raised him from infancy, passed away on June 25 from stomach cancer. Her death was followed four months later by Juel's grandfather Jens. After the deaths of his grandparents, Juel moved onto his father's Linden farm. Also living on the farm were his stepmother and her six children, as Frithjof had remarried in 1910. Like Frithjof, his second wife had also lost a spouse. Martine Ahlness was born in Norway in 1868. She was married to Andrew Bekken from 1889 until his passing in 1903. Juel was still listed as a household member on the farm when the 1920 U.S Census was taken.

Frithjof appears to have lived a quiet and humble existence. Very few records exist about his life. What is known is that, after decades of farming in Linden, and twenty years of marriage to Martine, Frithjof died of tuberculosis on January 21, 1929, at his Linden farmhouse. He had struggled with the terrible lung condition for ten years prior to his passing. The same disease that took his mother when he was six took his own life as well. He had arrived to Hanska as a ten-year-old boy, and stayed in the Hanska–Linden area his entire life. The Minnesota Deaths and Burials database states Frithjof was buried at Mount Pisquah Cemetery at the Nora Unitarian Church in Hanska, but his name doesn't appear on a current list of those buried there. The details of his burial remain a mystery.

Juel moved to Minneapolis as a young man, and the year following his father's death he married in Chisago County in 1930. He lived in the Minneapolis–St.Paul area for most of his adult life, where he had a long career with the United States Postal Service, retiring as a supervisor. He and his wife Mary Louise had one child in 1934; a son named Marvin.

Bernhard Gotfried Green
Gustav's 2nd Son, Reverend Green's Nephew
Born October 3, 1873

Reverend Green's next oldest nephew by Gustav was named Bernhard Gotfried. He was born in Oslo on October 3, 1873. He may have had only a few memories of his mother Fredrikke, who died shortly before Bernhard's fourth birthday. He was seven years old when he departed Norway on the *Angelo* and first arrived to Hanska, where he met his Uncle Lars for the first time in 1881. His early years in Minnesota were spent helping his father and brothers on the family farm in Hanska.

There should have been a double celebration on the day he turned ten years old, however fate's cruel hand interceded instead. His stepmother Andrea gave birth to his baby half-sister, Gina Amalie, on Bernard's tenth birthday. His new baby sister shared his birthday, but sadly, Andrea, died giving birth to her. And tragically, little Gina did not live to see her first birthday.

When he was twelve, his grieving father sold his farm to Bernard's Aunt Karen and returned to Norway. Bernard, like his brothers, was sent to work on area farms, but it's not known which farm he was placed with during his father's absence between 1885 and 1893. The 1890 U.S Census was destroyed, leaving many holes for historians.

The 1900 Census shows Bernhard was a boarder at buttermaker Anton Anderson's rented house in Hanska, working at Anderson's creamery as a manager. Martin Erickson, the Hanska postmaster, was also boarding with Anderson that year.

On June 29, 1900, Bernhard married his sweetheart, eighteen-year-old Anna Olsen Lokken, who was born in raised in Linden. The two were married by Revered Green at Linden Lutheran Church, just a few weeks after Bernhard's brother Frithjof's wedding was performed.

Bernhard and Annie's first daughter Cora Josephine was born in Linden two days before Christmas in 1901. In 1905, Bernhard was farming in Sigel, Brown County. He and Annie's second daughter Guida Jean, was born in November 1905 and baptized by Reverend Green at Lake Hanska Lutheran Church. After Guida was born, Bernhard was ready for a change and decided to relocate his family to northern Minnesota. He bought a farm in Greenbush, in Roseau County, to be closer to his father Gustav. His third daughter, Ada Gladys, was born in Greenbush in May 1910.

Unfortunately, Bernhard's beloved Annie passed away the following year in July 1911. She was buried at the Bethania Free Lutheran Cemetery in Greenbush, the same cemetery as her father-in-law Gustav. After her passing, Bernhard packed up his three little girls, the youngest only fourteen months old, and traveled back to Hanska where family and friends were available to help him raise his young daughters.

After returning home to Hanska, Bernhard had a year-long struggle with tuberculosis, eventually succumbing to the disease on June 28, 1916, six months after his father Gustav's death. He died one day before what would have been he and Annie's sixteenth wedding anniversary. Bernhard died of the same disease that took his mother when he was a little boy, and the same disease that would take his older brother Frithjof twelve years later. Annie's cause of death is unknown, but it's highly possible she died from tuberculosis as well.

Bernhard's passing at the young age of forty-two left his three daughters, ages fifteen, ten, and five orphaned. Two days after he died, Reverend Green traveled from his home in Minneapolis to perform the funeral service for his nephew at Linden Lutheran. During the blazing summer heat on the prairie, burials at that time were performed very soon after death. Bernhard is laid to rest in the church's cemetery. His obituary in the *New Ulm Post* states he was born in 1871. His tombstone in the Linden cemetery shows his birth year as 1872, and his marriage certificate lists his birthday in 1874. But none of these are correct. According to his baptismal records in Norway, he was baptized on October 6, 1873, at three days old.

Bernhard's obituary was listed in the *New Ulm Post* on July 7, 1916. It discussed his arrival to Brown County as a little boy thirty-five years prior, and his childhood spent on his father's homestead in the grove just east of Hanska. The article stated he was survived by his three daughters, his sister Clara, and his brothers Frithjof and Olaf. His brother Karl wasn't mentioned.

After Bernhard's unfortunate passing, Emma and Alfred Halvorsen of Madelia took in and raised his youngest daughter, Ada, when she was five years old. Because she was just a young child when both her parents died, Ada had no memory of her mother and few of her father. Her Aunt Emma was the sister of the girl's dearly departed mother Annie. The couple also had a two-year-old son who became a younger brother to Ada. Young Ada eventually began to go by the last name Halvorsen. According to her Uncle Alfred's obituary, he was known to be "an efficient farmer and a kind and considerate friend who was loyal to his hometown community and his church in Linden." Alfred and Emma are buried at Linden Lutheran Cemetery.

Four years after her father Bernhard's death, his oldest daughter Cora is listed as a boarder with Pastor Andrew Reece and his family in Madelia for the 1920 Census. Pastor Reece had taken over as lead pastor for Trinity Lutheran after Reverend Green retired. In the same 1920 Federal Censes, fourteen-year-old Guida Jean is listed as boarding with the widow Mary Iverson on 4th Street in Hanska.

Bernhard's two eldest daughters never married. Cora eventually moved to Los Angeles and worked for a photographer. She died in 1987, and is buried beside her father at Linden Lutheran Cemetery. Guida Jean became an elementary school teacher in Kanabec County, Minnesota. She retired in Minneapolis where she died at age sixty-seven, and is buried at Lakewood Cemetery in Minneapolis.

Ada, Bernhard's youngest daughter, graduated from Madelia High School in 1929 and moved to Winona, Minnesota, where she became a nurse. While living in Winona she met and married her husband, Walter Roloff. The couple moved to Los Angeles in the 1940s to be near Ada's sister Cora, but returned to Madelia later in life. Ada died in 1999 at the age of eighty-nine. She is buried alongside her husband Walter at Linden Lutheran Cemetery, with her father Bernhard and sister Cora buried nearby as well. Ada, like her two older sisters, never had any children, thus ending Bernhard's lineage.

Olaf Nicolai Green
Gustav's Third Son, Reverend Green's Nephew
February 14, 1875

Reverend Green's third nephew from Gustav was named Olaf Nicolai. According to his Norwegian baptism records, he was born on Valentine's Day, February 14, 1875 in Oslo. Like his brother Bernhard, it's possible he never knew his original birth date, because for the rest of his life all of his official paperwork states he was born on February 10 instead of the 14th.

Little Olaf was two-and-a-half years old when his mother Fredrikke died. He arrived to Hanska at the age of six, old enough to carry with him snippets of memories of Norway, the land of his birth. He lived on his father's homestead until Gustav returned to Norway when little Olaf was eleven.

Like his two older brothers, it's not known which farm he boarded with after his father left for Norway when he was a boy. Not much else is known of Olaf's childhood until the 1895 State census records. When he was twenty years old, Olaf was boarding with and working as a farm hand for Ole Christianson. Ole's farm was in neighboring Riverdale Township in Watonwan County, where he lived with his wife, six daughters, and young son. His second eldest daughter, thirteen-year-old Mattie, would later become Olaf's wife.

Five years later in 1900, Olaf was back in Hanska village living and working in town. He boarded with Nels J. Ouren and family. Mr. Ouren managed the Hanska Linden Cooperative Store where Olaf was employed as a salesman. He and Nels were friends and co-workers, as well as neighbors. They both bought lots close together on Summit Avenue, when the town was being expanded. Not only that, Olaf and his boss shared a love of music. Nels was the band leader of the Hanska Lake Shore Band, and Olaf sang in both the Trinity Lutheran and Linden Lutheran choirs. The following picture shows the Hanska Lake Shore Band around the turn of the century. While not confirmed, the horn player on the far left appears to be Olaf Green.

Hanska Lake Shore Band, circa 1905. Photo Credit: DougStephColby45 on www.ancestry.com

Olaf Green (?) Hanska Lake Shore Band, circa 1905.

It was during these days of hard work and play when Olaf married Ragna Matea "Mattie" Christianson on October 29, 1902, at Trinity Lutheran Church in Madelia. Mattie was a teenager when she fell in love with the farmhand Olaf, who worked for her father. Revered Green officiated the wedding. Olaf's brother Frithjof acted as a witness, as did his good friend Carl Christensen. The couple made their home in Hanska at 112 Summit Ave. It was in this house, built in 1900, where the couple's first four children were born: Gerald in 1903, Sadie in 1905, Morris in 1909, and Leonard in 1913. Leonard would grow up to bravely serve his country as a corporal in the U.S. Army during World War II.

House Built by Olaf Green 112 Summit Ave. Hanska, MN
Photo Credit: Author's Personal Collection.

In December 1908, The Modern Woodmen of Hanska, a fraternal society, elected new officers, and Olaf was re-elected as the organization's sentry. In 1910, Olaf was still working as a clerk at the general store, called the Farmer's Store. In March 1912, the city of Hanska held elections for town officers, and Olaf was elected as the town recorder. Around 1915, Olaf and Mattie left Hanska for Tordenskjold in Otter Tail County. This tiny township in northern Minnesota is where Olaf's youngest brother Carl was homesteading, and is where Olaf's family made their new home. Olaf and Mattie's youngest child Omer was born in Tordenskjold in 1917. The following year, in 1918, Olaf filled out his World War 1 draft card. On it he listed the following information: age: 43, build: medium, height: medium, hair: light, eyes: blue.

Farming life in Tordenskjold did not work out, and ten years after moving north the family returned to Madelia in 1925. Olaf had given up farming, and he and Mattie bought a house on Cross Street in town. The family attended Trinity Lutheran Church in Madelia. This is where the couple were married, and where their only daughter

Sadie Florence was married as well. Sadie married a boy she grew up with in Hanska named Burnis Nundahl in August 1926.

When Sadie's son was a toddler, and while she was pregnant with her second son, her father Olaf passed away at the age of fifty-three on May 8, 1928. There was a worldwide epidemic of encephalitis lethargic from 1916 to 1930. His obituary stated that he'd been ill with the disease for a period of five years, which is likely the reason for his retirement from farming, and why the family returned to Madelia. At the time of Olaf's death, the disease was referred to as "sleeping sickness," as stated on his death certificate.

His youngest sons were fifteen and ten years old when he passed. Olaf was buried in the Trinity Lutheran Cemetery, the same church he was married in and the same church he actively sang in. After his death, Mattie and their youngest two sons moved back to Otter Tail County, leaving the Madelia area for the last time. Brothers Olaf and Frithjof both died in their fifties within the same year. Olaf's obituary glowed with sentiments of what a kindly, highly-respected member of the community he was.

Olaf Green, Linden Lutheran Church Choir, circa 1910.

Karl Elvin Green
Gustav Green's Fourth Son, Reverend Green's Nephew
Born July 6, 1880

Karl Elvin was born on July 6, 1880, exactly three years to the day after his namesake brother Carl Ludwig was born. The first baby Carl passed away on the same day he was baptized at six weeks old at Grønland Church in Oslo. Ten other babies were baptized that day. Eighteen days later, Carl's mother Fredrikke succumbed to tuberculosis, leaving Gustav a widower with four young children. Mother and child were both buried at Grønland Cemetery, which no longer exists today.

After the loss of his wife and youngest son, the widower with four young children sought comfort with the widow Andrea Jakobsdatter from Lier in Akershus County. Although not yet married, Andrea became pregnant in 1879. Gustav married Andrea on September 5, 1880, at Østre Aker Church in Oslo, two months after the birth of their son Karl Elvin. Two weeks later, on September 19, little Karl was baptized at the same church.

Shortly after their wedding, preparations were made for the new family to immigrate to America. They left for the United States on March 30, 1881, when baby Karl was eight months old. Atlantic crossings were very dangerous for babies and small children due to the lack of sanitation and the crowded conditions the immigrants lived in. Karl and his four older siblings all arrived safely to Minnesota in the late spring of 1881.

All of the Norwegian church, census, and immigration records spell his name "Karl," but the spelling "Carl" was used exclusively after his immigration to America. For the remainder of his life, he also used "Edvin" as his middle name instead of his baptized "Elvin." Not only was the spelling of his name changed. For his entire lifetime, with the exception of his baptism record, his date of birth is noted as July 7, 1880. His true date of birth is July 6. He, like his brother Olaf, was likely unaware of his true birthday.

When he was two years old and his family was homesteading in Lake Hanska, Carl's baby sister Sigri Amelie was born in 1882. Sadly, the baby would live less than a year. The following year his mother Andrea died giving birth to his new baby sister, Gina Amalie. That baby sister would also pass away within the year.

With the loss of his mother and two baby sisters, Carl once again became the youngest of the siblings, and the only surviving child of Gustav by his departed wife Andrea. After Gustav buried his wife and daughters, signed permission for his oldest daughter Clara's marriage, and scattered his older sons to nearby farms, he gathered up five-year-old Carl and the two ventured back to Norway together.

Once home, Gustav married for a third time to Karoline Olsen. Gustav and Karoline had four children in quick succession. Ten-year-old Carl was not listed in the family home according to the 1891 Norway Census. He was being fostered by an elderly couple in Skedmo, perhaps as a hired boy, perhaps being rejected by his new stepmother.

When Carl was almost thirteen years old, his father Gustav settled his affairs in Norway and the newly blended family returned to America in 1893. The 1895 Minnesota State Census shows fifteen-year-old Carl as a laborer working on Ole P. Hougan's farm. It's not clear why he wasn't in the family home. Ole had a wife and three very young children, so the employment of young, strong help was likely needed for the farm to survive.

A few years later, Carl began working for the farm of recent widower Jacob Joramo. Jacob had employed his niece Mathea to run the household and care for Jacob's three young sons. Mathea was the daughter of Jacob's sister Marit. Jacob's fourth son, Joseph, was just a baby when his mother passed, so the boy was being raised by his grandparents, Knute and Sonva Lee, on their nearby farm.

While working on the farm, Mathea introduced Carl to her sister, Petra Johanne Torsdahl. Petra was Jacob Joramo's other niece. She was born January 23, 1881 in Linden, and was baptized, as were her ten siblings, by Reverend Green at Lake Hanska Lutheran Church.

Petra and Carl fell in love, and married on May 31, 1900. Carl's two older brothers, Frithjof and Bernhard, both married during June of that year as well. Frithjof and Bernhard were married in the church by their uncle Reverend Green, while Carl married Petra at the courthouse in New Ulm.

There is an interesting mystery on the 1900 Federal Census, taken two weeks after Carl's marriage to Petra. Their union is confirmed by county courthouse records, but on the census a few weeks later Carl is living on the Joramo farm with Petra's older sister Mathea, who was using the last name "Green."

Both Carl and Mathea state they are newly married on the census. The only marriage record found of Carl is to Petra in 1900, and the only marriage record found for Mathea is from 1902 in New Ulm. She married Theodore Erickson on her twenty-third birthday, February 8, 1902. Carl and Mathea were never a legally married couple. Petra, his true wife, is listed in the 1900 U.S. Census as newly married and living at her family's farm with her parents and younger siblings.

Speculating, perhaps Carl and Mathea were fearful of the census taker's opinion of the two, unmarried servants living in the same household. Or, perhaps the young friends were simply having a little bit of fun. History will never know. What is known is that both Carl and Petra, and Petra's sister Mathea and her husband Theodore, all had lifelong marriages. Both couples moved together to Ottertail County in northern Minnesota around the same time, so there were likely no ill-feelings involved.

Because Carl was the only brother of the four to be married in the courthouse and not by their uncle, perhaps the good reverend didn't approve of Carl and Mathea's unorthodox living situation. Mathea and Theodore also married at the courthouse and not in the church. Interestingly, and a testament to the close kinships within isolated farmsteads and small communities, all four of the Green brothers found their future brides through the farms they boarded with and worked on as young men when their father Gustav returned to Norway and left them in Hanska.

174

When Gustav and Karoline decided to relocate to Roseau County in northern Minnesota around the turn of the century, Carl and Petra did not join them. He stayed in Hanska and struggled to make a living during his young life by working as a farm hand and by doing odd jobs.

By 1910, Carl and Petra had moved to Candor in Otter Tail County. The 1912 plot map of Candor shows Carl and Petra owning a forty-acre homestead adjacent to Petra's mother Marit Trosdahl's one hundred and sixty acres. Interestingly, the map shows the farm in Marit's name instead of her husband Johan, who outlived her by eighteen years. When Marit died in 1915, she bequeathed $50 to each of her eleven children, including Petra.

Candor is approximately forty miles from Tordenskjold, the tiny township in Otter Tail County, where Carl's brother Olaf would relocate to around 1915. Forty miles from Candor, in the opposite direction of Tordenskjold, is Greenbush in Roseau County, where Carl's father Gustav and his several younger siblings lived as well. By the time Olaf arrived to Otter Tail County, Carl and Petra had moved once again. In 1912, the couple decided to try farming in Manitoba, Canada.

They couple crossed the U.S. border into Manitoba and became naturalized Canadian citizens in 1915. They made their home in the small township of Vassar, three miles from the U.S. border. Vassar, which translates to "water" in German, was a tiny township first inhabited in 1896 with the arrival of the newly laid railroad. Unlike Hanska, there was not a large population of Norwegian immigrants who settled in Vassar. Most citizens were predominantly French Catholics.

Carl and Petra were never blessed with children. They lived simply. He does not appear in any census records past 1931, but the 1931 Canadian Census shows that Carl was able to have purchased a humble house. It shows his home was worth $100, had two bedrooms, and was made of wood. He spoke English, did not speak French, and his native tongue was Norwegian.

Carl passed away on September 12, 1956. Canada does not publicly post death records until seventy years have passed, and because he and Petra left no descendants, his cause of death is unknown. Unlike his older brothers who died in their forties and fifties, Carl lived a long life of seventy-six years. Petra died fifteen year later in 1971, and both are buried at the Hillside Lutheran Cemetery in Vassar. For a poor, struggling farmer who had so little wealth during his lifetime, he is laid to rest with a large, tall, headstone and a slab footstone to mark his existence in the world.

Of the four sons of Gustav who immigrated in 1881, Carl was unique. Of Gustav's twenty-one children, Carl was the only surviving child of Gustav's second wife Andrea. Carl was the only child Gustav brought back to Norway with him to marry Caroline and start another family before returning to Hanska. He was the only sibling to immigrate to Canada, and the only sibling who never had children. Further, he was not listed as a surviving sibling in the obituary of his brother Bernhard. It could have easily been an oversight, or there could have been a falling out of sorts. Like his brother Bernhard, whose daughters never had children, Carl's familial line stopped with him.

Gina Birgitte Green Christiansen
Reverend Green's Niece, Grandpa Rolf's Aunt
Born August 25, 1865

The first of Reverend Green's family to arrive in Minnesota was his teenage niece, Gina. Seven years after he and his wife Jensine had been settled in the Hanska–Madelia area, the reverend brought fourteen-year-old Gina to live with them and to help Jennie with the children. She arrived in the spring of 1880, a year before her brother Axel and her uncle Gustav's family arrived.

Gina's father Bernt was Reverend Green's older brother. Bernt lost his wife in December of 1879 when she was forty-seven years old. Her death left behind five children. After she passed, all the children, with the exception of the youngest son who was only ten years old at her passing, ended up leaving home for a new life in

176

Minnesota. Six months after her mother's passing, Gina Birgitte was almost fifteen when she appeared in the June 1880 U.S. Census. She is listed as "niece," living in the household of Reverend Green in Madelia.

Considering it took four to six weeks for letters of news to pass between the States and Norway; it appears that arrangements were either in place prior to her mother's passing or immediately afterward. It's difficult to image in today's world, a fourteen-year-old girl having the bravery and fortitude to travel solo for several weeks across the ocean with little money and few belongings, and then continue those travels by train to a new land, with no way to call home for help if needed.

A fire at the U.S. Department of Commerce in January 1921 destroyed most of the 1890 Federal Census records. Because of that, not much information is known about Gina's life between arriving to Madelia in 1880 and her marriage to Ole Christiansen on July 1, 1891. Ole Christiansen was a very common Norwegian name. Her husband is not the Ole Christensen Gina's cousin Olaf boarded with in Riverdale Township.

Gina and Ole were married in Menomonie, Wisconsin, a small town in Dunn County, a few miles from where Gina's brother Axel and cousin Clara moved to in 1886. It's likely that Gina relocated from Hanska to Dunn County with her brother when he and Clara left the area. Gina and Clara were relatively close in age, and likely formed a deep friendship. The couple's first child, a girl they named Beryl, was born in Wisconsin on September 17, 1893. Gina had another daughter, Hedvig, in 1899. A few years later, Gina and Ole moved to Portland, Oregon, where their third and last daughter Olga was born in 1905.

Gina and Ole lived in Portland for the remainder of their lives. Gina's sister Emma would later join her in the Portland area during the 1920s. Gina was one of the last of her generation who could tell the tale of sailing solo across the ocean as a teenager, homesteading the prairie with horse and wagon, and then relocating to a large metropolis with all the modern conveniences of the 1950s. Gina

Birgitte Green Christiansen lived a long and amazing life and died at age ninety-four in Portland on March 3, 1959.

Emma Bolette Green Olby
Reverend Green's Niece, Grandpa Rolf's Aunt
Born July 22, 1863

Two years after Gustav and his family arrived, another set of relatives headed toward the American Midwest, but instead of Minnesota, their destination was to Menomonie, Wisconsin. On May 31, 1883, the steamship *Thingvalla* departed Oslo Harbor. On board were Gina and Axel Green's two teenaged siblings: Emma, age nineteen, and her brother Lars, age sixteen.

Their sister Gina, who was born between the two siblings, was the first to arrive in 1880 when she was fourteen. Their brother Axel would arrive in 1881 with Gustav's family on the *Angelo*. The only child of their father Bernt and his first wife not to immigrate was their youngest sibling, fourteen-year-old Bernt Junior, who stayed in Norway and never immigrated. After the loss of his mother, perhaps the boy felt a duty to stay behind and care for their father (and inherit the farm) after all the other siblings decided to immigrate. Their father, Bernt Senior, remarried and had six more children.*

Bernt's youngest son Guul was born in 1896 when Bernt was sixty-two-years-old. Guul is the father of Rolf, and the great-grandfather of the author of this book.

Onboard *Thingvalla* with them was Emma's future husband Gotfred Olby, who was from their same village of Mødum. Gotfred was six years older than Emma. He was born Gotfred Olsen, but took the name Olby, a derivative of Olafsby, his family farm. The two knew each other from back home. They had either decided to run away together to America, or they had formed a connection during the crossing on their way to start their new lives.

Gotfred and Emma were married in Menomonie, Wisconsin on September 21, 1883, three months after arriving in America. They were married at Our Saviour's Lutheran Church. Reverend Green was a witness, but did not officiate. Seven months after their marriage,

Emma gave birth to her and Gotfred's first child. It's unknown why her Uncle Lars traveled all the way to Wisconsin with them to witness the marriage, but not to officiate in either there or in Brown County. Perhaps he knew of his niece's pregnancy and wanted to support the couple, but could not ethically perform the ceremony. From his writings he was undoubtedly a very pious man. Serendipitously, Emma and Gotfred's daughter was born on April 20, 1884, Reverend Green's forty-third birthday. Emma named her Gonnor after her departed mother.

The young family eventually headed north to Ashland to be with extended family—Clara, Axel, and brother Lars. In 1906, Emma's twenty-two-year-old daughter Gonnor ventured west from Wisconsin to Portland, Oregon. Emma's sister Gina had relocated to Portland around the same time, so it was likely a comfort to Emma to know her daughter was safe with her aunt. Once in Portland, Gonnor married a Swedish farmer named Oscar Nils Wallin.

Sometime in the 1920s, when Emma and Gotfred entered their retirement years, they also moved west to Portland where they would spend the rest of their lives. The couple had a total of ten children, half of whom also migrated to Portland. Emma died at age sixty-five in her home at 906 South Syracuse Street on March 29, 1929. Her cause of death was from chronic diabetes and a severe ear infection. Gotfred died a few years later in 1932. The couple are buried together at Columbian Pioneer Cemetery in Portland.

Lars Gustav Green
Revered Green's Nephew and Namesake, Grandpa Rolf's Uncle
Born March 30, 1867

Lars Gustav Green was named after his two uncles, Lars and Gustav. He was born one year after Reverend Green left for America. His early days were spent working on the family farm at Grinkelsrud. His father Bernt, as well as his uncle Gustav, were both highly skilled bakers. Lars' mother died in 1879. When he was thirteen, his sister Gina immigrated soon after their mother's passing to live with their uncle in Madelia. The following year, on Lars' fourteenth birthday, his brother Axel left for America as well. Not wanting to be left behind by their older siblings, young Lars and sister Emma decided to make the journey as well.

Shortly after his sixteenth birthday, Lars and his nineteen-year-old sister Emma, boarded the steamer *Thingvalla* and departed Oslo for America on May 31, 1883. On board with him and Emma was a friend of his from Mødum, as well as Gotfred Olby, who would marry Emma shortly after landing. On the ship manifest Lars was listed next to Gotfred as "boy." Perhaps he was hired to be Gotfred's assistant.

The ship stopped for a few weeks in Copenhagen, Denmark, before continuing the journey across the Atlantic on June 21, 1883. The 321 immigrant passengers arrived in New York, and the group began the overland journey to Wisconsin. It's not known if they briefly stopped in Hanska to see family first before continuing their journey north. If they did stop to visit, they would have then taken the train from New Ulm to Minneapolis, then a straight shot from Minneapolis to Menomonie.

Young Lars did not want to be a farmer like most of the men in his family. He chose to settle in Ashland, Wisconsin, to be near his brother Axel and cousin Clara. Axel worked for the railroad and was able to help his little brother get a job with him as a brakeman with the Chicago & Northwestern Railroad Company.

Lars met and fell in love with a young woman named Julia Brown. The two were married on April 8, 1889, in Eau Claire, Wisconsin, when they were both twenty-two years old. The young couple soon started a family. Unfortunately, their lives together would be brief. While working as a brakeman on the railroad, Lars died a week before his twenty-seventh birthday on March 22, 1894.

His tragic death by typhoid fever left Julia a young widow with two sons, both under the age of two. Julia sued the Ashland Water District. She claimed Lars died from drinking contaminated city water. The case was tried before the Wisconsin Supreme Court. It was the first case of its kind, and it was of interest to the entire country. She won her case in the Wisconsin Supreme Court and was awarded $5000. The news made several local and national newspapers, and water safety regulations were put in place due to his passing. Lars is buried at Mount Hope Cemetery in Ashland, Wisconsin.

Karen Green Asleson
Reverend Green's Sister, Grandpa Rolf's Great-Aunt
Born January 15, 1844

Reverend Green was the fourth child born to his parents. His brother Gustav was the seventh, and born between the two brothers were three sisters including twins, Karen and Edda Birgitte. The twin girls were born during a frozen Norwegian winter on January 15, 1844. The siblings, so close in age, no doubt had countless fond childhood memories of growing up on Grinkelsrud farm. Like her brother Lars, Karen was not baptized with a middle name. Lars used "Engebretsen" as his middle name, and Karen used "Engebretsdatter" as hers.

Of the Green family's ten children, the four middle siblings Lars, Karen, Gustav, and Olava all immigrated to America. The two oldest brothers, Ole and Bernt, never left Norway. Nor did the family's eldest daughter Bertha, Karen's twin Edda, or the youngest two sisters Ida and Berte. Perhaps these four middle siblings, being the closest in age, had a deep bond that oceans couldn't separate.

Karen's twin, Edda Birgitte, married young and stayed in Norway her entire life. When Karen was still unmarried at age thirty-seven, she, along with younger sister Maren Olava, decided to immigrate to America. The two sisters joined their brother Gustav, his wife Andrea, their five children, and her nephew Axel aboard the *Angelo* on March 30, 1881. One can imagine the two sisters standing at the railing of the sailing ship, steadfastly holding hands as they departed the harbor. They watched the shores of Norway disappear as the ship steamed into the vastness of the ocean. Karen would never see her twin sister or Norway again.

Almost three years to the day after arriving in Hanska, Karen married Ellef Asleson at Trinity Lutheran Church in Madelia. Ellef was from neighboring Buskerud County back home in Norway. Reverend Green officiated his sister's wedding on March 29, 1884. Ellef was a widower. He had been caring for his three small children since his wife died the previous year. Once married, Karen became mother to Ellef's son Anton, age nine, daughter Gena, age eight, and little Ole who was just three years old. Karen and Ellef never had children of their own.

The 1885 Minnesota Census lists Ellef and Karen as farming their land in Hanska, and Gustav is the very next farm in the census. Ellef owned a huge track of land along where the railroad tracks would be in Hanska, as well as other rural plots. County records show Ellef Asleson purchased his brother-in-law Gustav's homestead in November 1885, just prior to Gustav's temporary return to Norway.

The *New Ulm Review* posted in February 1887 that Ellef and Karen owned at least 240 acres in Hanska. Ellef had purchased additional, adjacent land besides what he bought from Gustav.

The following images show the land owned by Karen's brother Gustav Green in 1881, shortly after arriving for the first time, compared to the land owned by Ellef and Karen Asleson in 1905 (the white area of the image). They appear to overlap.

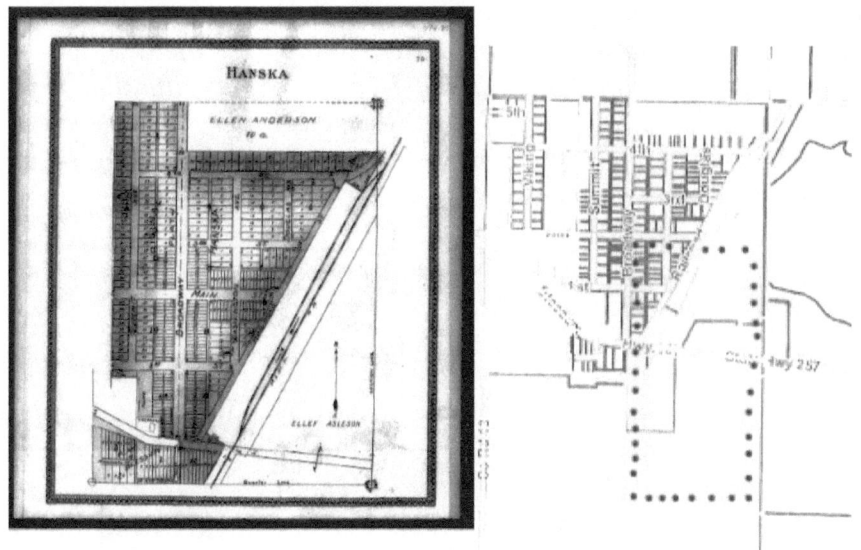

Karen and Ellef Asleson Land, 1905   Gustav Green Land, 1881
(the white area, right side)   (highlighted)

In the spring of 1893, Gustav returned to Hanska. He had gone home to Norway for eight years, and upon his return he rented his former land back from his sister. Newspapers of bygone eras used to post the life events and happenings of its community members. The November 29, 1893 edition of the *New Ulm Review* read: "Ellef Asleson has rented his farm to G. Green and sons for a term of five years." Gustav would however leave three-and-a-half years after the lease agreement to purchase his own homestead in Greenbush, Minnesota. His departure left the running of the rented farm to his sons.

On August 23, 1893, the *New Ulm Review* posted an article about a terrible accident that happened on Karen and Ellef's farm to a twenty-seven-year-old, Norwegian immigrant farm hand.

A friend of J. P. Bolstad, who came here recently from the Northern part of the state, Conrad Bang by name, met with a serious accident near town last Friday afternoon while running a traction engine for Ellef Asleson of Lake Hanska. He was in some way caught between the engine and separator and badly crushed. He was brought to town and given over to the care of Dr. Hirsch. Though his life was at first despaired of, he is still living, though in a precarious situation.

The young man would survive his tragic injury and go on to live a long life of eighty-nine years.

As mentioned previously in this book, the 1890 Federal Census was destroyed, but subsequent censuses show Karen and Ellef farming their land in 1895 and 1900.

In the summer of 1899, the railroad was at last being expanded towards Linden and Hanska. The railroad workers camped on Olaf Haubakken's farm, and another crew on Iver Stone's farm. The June 21, 1899 edition of the *New Ulm Review* posted the following announcement about the incoming Minneapolis & St. Louis Railroad:

It is not decided where the station will be located in Hanska. It is rumored that the Railroad Co. has offered Mr. Ellef Asleson $45 an acre for his 80 acres east of the track, but Mr. Asleson is holding out for a higher price. If a settlement cannot be brought about, the station will be on Jacob Joramo's farm.

Five years later in June 1905, Ellef had switched his occupation from "farmer" to "landlord" on the state census. Ellef was in poor health and was no longer able to perform the laborious farm work. He passed away six months later, a few days after Christmas, on December 28, 1905. His burial five days later on January 2, 1906 is registered at Lake Hanska Lutheran Church. He was sixty years old.

After her husband's death, Karen moved into the home of her stepdaughter Gena, and Gena's husband Anton Brudeli. In 1910, when she was sixty-six years, old Karen lived with the family in their house at 109 Broadway Street, which is today the address of the Hanska Community Library. Gena managed a small restaurant on the town's main street while Karen looked after the two grandchildren. Ten years later, the family was again living on their farm in Linden, and there were then five grandchildren to keep her busy.

The last census Karen was listed in was in 1930. She was eighty-six-years old and still living with Gena and Anton. Karen Green Asleson died on May 2, 1934, at the Linden farmhouse. She lived a long, amazing life of ninety years. Like many of her generation, she went from rural farm life in Norway with no modern conveniences, to sailing across an ocean to an unknown land. In her ninety years, she saw the invention of the railroad make its way to her own backyard. She was present when radio, household electricity and plumbing, and automobiles became commonplace. Her cause of death and burial records could not be found, but she was most likely buried at Lake Hanska Lutheran Cemetery with her husband Ellef.

Karen's stepdaughter Gena, as well as Gena's husband Anton, are both buried at Zion Lutheran Church Cemetery where they were active members. Anton died in September 1942, and Gena followed six months later on March 4, 1943 of cancer. Gena's obituary shares how she cherished happy memories of growing up on the Linden farm. She owned a small restaurant in the village for a short while around 1903, and she loved flowers and gardening. She was known to be a very kind woman who would be greatly missed within the community.

Karen's eldest step-son, Anton, is also buried at Zion Lutheran Cemetery. It's unknown where the youngest of the three siblings, Ole, is buried, but Ole's son Russell and grandson Ozzie were also active members of Zion Lutheran Church in Hanska and are buried in the church cemetery.

When the author's family lived in Hanska, they unknowingly lived two houses down from the widow of Ole Asleson's grandson.

Maren "Olava" Green Olsen
Reverend Green's Sister, Grandpa Rolf's Great-Aunt
Born June 23, 1849

Reverend Green's youngest sibling to journey from Norway to join him in Minnesota was his sister Maren Olava Green. She was the eighth child of their parents Embret and Barbo to be born on the

185

family farm Grinkelsrud. Early in life, she dropped her first name and went almost exclusively by her middle name "Olava." She was almost thirty-two-years old when she immigrated to America on March 30, 1881, aboard the *Angelo*. Also on board the ship with her were her sister Karen, brother Gustav, Gustav's young family, and her nephew Axel.

Less than a year after being settled in Minnesota, Olava married her husband Sigvart Olsen on April 13, 1882. They were married at Bethlehem Lutheran Church in Mankato, Minnesota. Mankato is within Blue Earth County, which neighbors Brown and Watonwan Counties. The couple bought a house and settled in Mankato, where they stayed for most of their lives.

Although she was an older bride for that time, their union was blessed with four children. Their daughter Emma was born in 1883, their son Oscar in 1885, daughter Jessie in 1888, followed by their youngest Wilhelmina "Minnie" in 1890. All their children were baptized at Bethlehem Lutheran in Mankato where the family was active members.

Olava's husband, Sigvart Olsen, was also from Akershus County. It's not known if they knew each other from back home and planned a life together in America or if this was a coincidence, but records indicate they most likely made a plan. Sigvart immigrated first. He left the shores of Oslo on February 20, 1881, aboard the ship *Kelso*. He immigrated solo as a young man of twenty-five-years. He was seven years younger than his future bride, Olava.

It's unknown why Sigvart didn't join Olava and the Green family, who departed only a month after him. Since "Olsen" was such a common name for immigrants, deeper research was conducted to make sure it was the same Sigvart Olsen who immigrated from Akershus a month before Olava. The following details show it most likely was: as a married couple both Sigvart and Olava state "1881" as their year of immigration on all U.S. Censuses, his listed age on the passenger list matches his year of birth, both Olava and Sigvart used the agent M. A. Lea, and both stated their destination was La Crosse, Wisconsin.

Sigvart made a living as a craftsman stonecutter. In 1900, the couple lived at their owned home at 723 East Warren Street in Mankato. By 1910, they purchased a new home and moved to 413 Glenwood Street in Mankato. The family had a maid, who was a recent immigrant from Norway named Sigreid Olsen. It's unknown if she was a family member from the old country, or if the same last name was just a coincidence.

The 1910 census gives further detailed information about the family. Both Olava and Sigvart spoke, read, and wrote English, although their mother tongue was Norwegian. All their children were gainfully employed. Their oldest daughter Emma worked as a clerk in the county auditor's office. Oscar was employed as a tailor, Jessie was a clerk for a judge probate, and Minnie was a school teacher.

The grown children had moved on by the 1920 census, but Olava and Sigvart were in their same house on Glenwood Street. Sixty-four-year-old Sigvart was still working as a stonecutter, and Olava kept house. Their youngest three children had moved to the Twin Cities to raise families of their own, but unfortunately, their eldest daughter Emma Amelia died in 1918, possibly of the Spanish Flu. Emma never married, nor had children, and is buried at Mount Olivet Cemetery in Mankato.

The 1920 census was the last one where Sigvart and Olava would be listed. Sigvart, a hardworking man into his later years, passed away on April 25, 1925. Olava lived another four years after her husband's passing. She died on June 10, 1929, two weeks before her eightieth birthday. Olava and Sigvart were married for forty-three years before they were separated by death. They are buried together at Mount Olivet Cemetery in Mankato along with their eldest daughter, Emma.

The Ships

SS *Bothnia*. 1874. Photo Credit: Maritime Museum Liverpool.
https://www.liverpoolmuseums.org.uk/artifact/photograph-of-bothnia-cunard-line

Characters to themselves in the story of the Green Family from Norway are the sailboats and steamers that bridged the gap between the old world and the new. They carried not only thousands of scared, penniless immigrants within their steel hulls—they carried thousands of dreams as well. For weeks on end, they were held steady at the helm by the skilled seamen. The sturdy steamers protected her many travelers from the wind and waves of the mighty Atlantic Ocean.

SS Angelo was built in 1874 in Hull, England, and was first launched that same year. Her builders were Humphrey & Pearson, and she was operated by the Wilson Line. She was 258 feet long, thirty-three feet wide, and eighteen feet high: small compared to today's massive ships, but a magnificent marvel to her passengers.

She was built to carry Scandinavian emigrants on the first leg of their journey from Oslo to Hull. The ship departed weekly, every Friday, and the voyage took approximately two days. From Hull, emigrants would travel three hours by train to Liverpool, then board another ship for the final leg to New York. Once in New York, travelers would either disembark, or, if they were headed to the Midwest, would continue the journey through the Great Lakes into Wisconsin.

Reverend Lars Green left Norway in 1866 aboard a three-masted sailing vessel. Within a few years time, by 1870, nearly ninety percent of immigrants arrived to America by steamship rather than sail. The *SS Angelo* wasn't only a safe and functional vessel; she was built with comfort and beauty in mind as well. Her accommodations were built for both first class and steerage, both of which were superior for the time. Besides the dormitories and staterooms, she also had a large dining hall, drawing room, smoking room, reading room, and even a separate saloon for the ladies.

In the book *The Wilson Line of Hull, 1831–1981* by Arthur G. Credland & M. Thompson, there is a description of the *SS Angelo's* interior drawing room:

> *...the upholstery is green velvet, which offers a fine contrast of color with the gilded carved work. The sofas are fixed across each end and the front side of the place reserved for a Broadwood piano. The floor is covered with a velvet pile carpet, of rich pink and blue pattern. Altogether the drawing room is most elegant and affords a degree of comfort and convenience rarely attained on board ship.*

SS Angelo's last voyage was on November 10, 1905. After 700 voyages of shuttling thousands of immigrants from Norway to England, her years had come to an end. She was sold for scrap in February 1906.

The Green Family boarded the *SS Angelo* on March 30, 1881. Two days later they arrived in Hull, England. From there the family of ten took the train to Liverpool, where they'd have a brief stay before the next leg of their journey. A week later, the family boarded the *SS Bothnia* on April 9, 1881.

SS Bothnia was built in 1874 in Glasgow, Scotland. She was built the same year as the *SS Angelo*, but *SS Bothnia* was much larger. She was four hundred and twenty-two feet long, forty-two feet wide, and thirty-four feet high. She was operated by the Cunard Line. She had two sister ships: *SS Gallia* and *SS Scythia*. The *Bothnia*'s built purpose was as a trans-Atlantic immigrant ship for immigrants between Liverpool and New York.

Not much specific information in known about the *Bothnia,* but life aboard an immigrant ship was no easy endeavor for its passengers. The voyage across the Atlantic took approximately ten days. Passengers were required to bring their own utensils and bedding. Prior to boarding, passengers were organized into groups of six to ten. Within their group they would receive their rations, cook their meals, and eat together as a group. The Green Family's party of ten likely formed their own mess group. Meals consisted of oats, rice porridge, meat pies, and pea soup. Passengers were required to clean their berths, and inspections took place to make sure all was in order. Religious services were held, and laundry could only be done on the scheduled day. During the leisure time of the afternoon, passengers could wander about the ship, and many spent the time to read, sew, or write letters home.

The Green Family's voyage took twenty days from when they left the shores of Norway until they arrived in New York Harbor. As if the hand of God was safely guiding the family to their beloved brother and uncle, the day they arrived was a particularly special one. The ten weary passengers first set foot upon American soil on Reverend Green's fortieth birthday, April 20, 1881.

SS Stavangerfjord, 1954. Photo Credit: Author's Personal Collection.

The last members of the Green family left Norway to start a new life in the United States eighty-eight years after Reverend Lars embarked on his journey. My grandparents, Rolf and Unni, were married on May 8, 1954. Four days later, on May 12, the twenty-two-year-olds boarded the *SS Stavangerfjord* and waved farewell to their families and friends.

The ocean liner that brought them across the Atlantic was first put into service in April of 1918, when it sailed to New York. Because of the World War, it took five months for it to return to Bergen, Norway. The *Stavangerfjord* was built in Birkenhead, England, and was sixty-four feet wide and five hundred and thirty-two feet long. Originally built to be fueled by coal, she was converted to oil combustion in 1924.

In 1940, the Germans invaded Norway and seized the *Stavangerfjord* while she was anchored in Oslo Harbor. The enemy used her as a supply ship for the duration of World War II. Following the war, the ship resumed her transatlantic passenger crossings. She was retrofitted with one hundred and twenty-two first-class cabins, two hundred and twenty-two cabin-class cabins, and three hundred and thirty-five tourist-class cabins—the most economic option. I asked my grandfather which level they had and he didn't remember, but said with a smile, "I don't think it was first class."

Two tickets for the couple cost them 2400 NOK, which equated to roughly $300 USD at that time. This equates to around $3500 in 2025 currency rates. The ship provided entertainment during the journey—shows and dancing—but because the weather was so lovely, the young couple spent most of their time strolling the deck. All-you-can-eat Smorgasbord meals, served buffet style, were included with the price of the tickets.

While on deck one day, Rolf recognized an acquaintance from back home, Odd Fausko, whose grandfather lived up the road from Rolf's family. Odd was traveling solo, headed to Fargo, North Dakota to work as a salesman. After bumping into Odd, Unni also ran into someone she knew. She recognized a classmate from her school days in Oslo—a young woman named Solveig. In his retelling, Rolf said "It's a small world. . . and a small country." Everyone exchanged information to keep in touch.

The crossing took eight days. The *Stavangerfjord* first stopped in Halifax, Nova Scotia, to let the passengers who were destined for Canada depart before continuing on to New York Harbor. Rolf and Unni were destined for Canada as well, specifically Montreal, Quebec, but the young honeymooners wanted to see New York City first.

All the passengers were lined upon the deck that beautiful, sunny afternoon in May to witness the Statue of Liberty welcome them all to America. Known as the "Old Lady," the *SS Stavangerfjord* faithfully continued her Atlantic crossings until 1964, when she was eventually sold for scrap. The days of immigrants arriving by ship came to an end as air travel replaced ocean travel.

Rolf and Unni had $100 in their pocket when they first set foot in America—poor and eager, with their entire future ahead of them, just as the Greens of the nineteenth century were when they landed generations earlier. The young couple spent three days touring the Big Apple before they took a train to Montreal, where they would settle for a few years.

My mother, Monica, was born in Montreal in 1955. From there they moved to Vancouver, British Columbia, and reached out to their old friend Odd Fausko. He was working as a plumber in Seattle, and told Rolf that his landlady would agree to sponsor the young family to come to the United States. Rolf and Unni settled in Seattle, had two sons after Monica, and created a prosperous and successful life for themselves. They lived the American Dream.

The ships that brought our grandparents to America are a part of all of our stories—our nation's story. Crowded within their wooden and steel hulls were the millions of people who carried little with them except their dreams and determination. They carried with them not only their histories, but their future legacies as well. They made us who we are today.

Rolf and Unni Green. May 12, 1954. Boarding the *SS Stavangerfjord* for America
after their wedding on May 8, 1954. Photo Credit: Author's Personal Collection

Special Thanks

I need to thank the following people, who without them, this book would not have been possible. I am forever grateful for your support, knowledge, and passion for keeping the history of Brown County and the stories of our Norwegian immigrant pioneers alive for future generations.

❀   My husband Noah and sons Ethan and Sam—you are my world.

❀   Joel Botten, Carol and Alan Thormodson, Larry Harbo, Randy Paulson, Barb Overlie, and all the Friends of Linden Lutheran Church and Cemetery Association.

❀   The Brown County Historical Society in New Ulm, MN.

❀   The Watonwan County Historical Society in Madelia, MN.

❀   E. Maxwell Moore, my brilliant editor.

❀   Joe Green, great-grandson of Reverend Lars Green and fellow family historian.

❀   Cathy Lundeen, Archivist for Collections & Records Management, Evangelical Lutheran Church in America (ELCA)

About the Author

Kristen S. Moore spends her time between her homes in Bremerton, Washington and Hanska, Minnesota. She graduated from Washington State University with a Bachelor's of Arts degree in Social Science and a minor in history, and later graduated from nursing school at Olympic College in Bremerton, Washington. She is married to her high school sweetheart and love of her life, Noah. She and her husband have two adult sons and an elderly cat named Mouse. She lives a quiet and peaceful life while enjoying her passions of writing, history, traveling, and cooking. Reverend Lars E. Green was the brother of her great-great-grandfather.

Thank you for reading

By the Grace of God

The Story of Reverend Lars E. Green

If you've enjoyed this book please consider writing a positive review
on Amazon, Barnes & Noble, Goodreads, or another platform of your
choosing. Your feedback is immensely valuable in helping
independent authors like us reach a wider audience.

If you'd like to order additional copies for yourself, your friends, and
your family, it can be ordered on Amazon, Barnes & Noble, major
retailers, or you can request a copy at your local library and
independent bookstores. J

Purchasing directly from the publisher's website at
www.otterhousebooks.com
provides the best support to the author.

OTTERHOUSE
BOOKS

www.ingramcontent.com/pod-product-compliance
Lightning Source LLC
Chambersburg PA
CBHW021144130626
46554CB00005B/1655